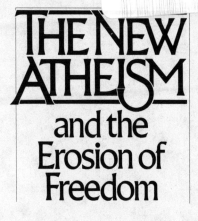

THE NEW ATHEISM
and the Erosion of Freedom

THE NEW ATHEISM

and the Erosion of Freedom

ROBERT A. MOREY

BETHANY HOUSE PUBLISHERS
MINNEAPOLIS, MINNESOTA 55438
A Division of Bethany Fellowship, Inc.

Published by Bethany House Publishers
A Division of Bethany Fellowship, Inc.
6820 Auto Club Road, Minneapolis, Minnesota 55438

Printed in the United States of America

Library of Congress Cataloging-in-Publication Data

Morey, Robert A., 1946-
   The new atheism and the erosion of freedom.

   Bibliography: p.
   1. Atheism—Controversial literature.   2. Christianity and atheism.   3. Religious liberty.   4. Apologetics—20th century.   I. Title.
BL2747.3.M567   1986   239′.7   86-8261
ISBN 0-87123-889-6 (pbk.)

Preface

The 20th Century has been called the century of the atheist. With the disastrous success of Communism in the East and the devastating impact of Humanism in the West, atheism has become the religion of the modern unbelieving man. It is organized, armed and determined to extirpate all vestiges of religious belief from the world. Our modern educational system and mass media reflect this completely secularized and godless new world.

Though once a quaint anachronism, atheism has today become a force which Christians must take with the utmost seriousness; therefore, I was particularly delighted to see Dr. Robert A. Morey's excellent new work. In this readable and understandable volume, Dr. Morey reveals the fallacies and failures of materialistic atheism. It is *must* reading not only for Christians, but for all of those that hold dear the culture of Western civilization.

D. James Kennedy
Senior Pastor of
Coral Ridge Presbyterian Church

Dr. Robert Morey has earned degrees in philosophy, theology and apologetics. He is listed in *The International Authors and Writers Who's Who*, and *Contemporary Writers* and is presently Executive Director of the Research and Education Foundation. His books (some have been translated into Spanish, German, French and Chinese) include:

Death and the Afterlife
When Is It Right to Fight?
A Christian Handbook for Defending the Faith
Horoscopes and the Christian
Reincarnation and Christianity
How to Answer a Mormon
How to Answer a Jehovah's Witness
The Saving Work of Christ
Worship Is All of Life
The Bible and Drug Abuse
The Dooyeweerdian Concept of the Word of God
An Examination of Exclusive Psalmody
Is Sunday the Christian Sabbath?
Outlines for Living

Table of Contents

Introduction 9
Chapter One: The Crazy Sixties 11
Chapter Two: The Erosion of Freedom 16
Chapter Three: The New Atheism 25
Chapter Four: Defining Atheism 38
Chapter Five: The Causes of Atheism 51
Chapter Six: Logic and the Atheists 62
Chapter Seven: Logical Errors of Atheism 72
Chapter Eight: Materialism 90
Chapter Nine: A Sample Debate 107
Chapter Ten: Jesus and Paul 135
Chapter Eleven: Atheists in Action 141
Conclusion 160
Appendix: Answers to Common Objections 161
Bibliography 170

Introduction

Every philosophical viewpoint, or world and life view, has its own fulcrum upon which all its meaning balances. The entire system rests on this one pivotal idea. If this idea can be disproven, nothing else in the system has any meaning. Like a house of cards, if the bottom card is removed, the entire house comes tumbling down in ruin.

The secular humanists have applied this philosophical approach to Christianity for years, rightly acknowledging that the existence of God is the Archimedean point of the Christian world and life view. Everything that Christianity teaches rests entirely on the existence of God. Therefore, instead of trying to disprove the Christian system on every point, the humanists have labored to refute the existence of God. Once the existence of God can be disproven, then the Christian system is destroyed.

This approach should be applied to all systems of thought, including the humanists'. While they have pressed this issue with the theists for several centuries, they remarkably have escaped analysis of *their* Archimedean point: the belief that they have refuted the existence of God and therefore can declare there is no God. Upon this foundation they develop their morals, values and priorities.

Because humanism depends on God's nonexistence, the "soul" of humanism is atheism. Just as Christianity pivots on the existence of God, humanism pivots on the nonexistence of God. Everything that humanism teaches is a development or an application of the nonexistence of God. And this process rests entirely upon their refutation of the existence of God. If this one point is proven erroneous, then the entire system of humanism collapses.

In this light we have the right to ask some questions:

1. Have the humanists successfully refuted the existence of God, the integrity of the Bible, the historicity of Jesus, and the validity of Christianity—as they claim?

2. Are their arguments *logically* valid in their structure and form?

3. Are their arguments *verified* by historical or scientific facts?

Since secular humanism depends on its claim that it has refuted theism, if its arguments are found logically invalid, and historically and scientifically erroneous, then humanism has no meaning. If humanism has failed to prove the nonexistence of God, then it has also failed to prove its first principle, its starting point—that there is no God. Everything in the system rests on this pivotal point.

This book makes a logical analysis of the typical arguments advanced by modern atheists, skeptics, freethinkers, agnostics, etc., who claim they have successfully refuted the existence of God in one way or another. Since secular humanism is based on atheism, a critical study of the origin and nature of modern atheism and unbelief is the best way to confront this philosophy.

For many years atheistic humanists have played the game of logical argument. We will now play it too; with their rules; on their turf; for an eternal prize.

1

The Crazy Sixties

At the beginning of the turbulent sixties, atheists and other infidels were so few in number that Chicago theologian Martin Marty confidently wrote:

> He [the infidel] was no longer with us. As early as the first years of this century denominational periodicals noted his passing. Today "infidelity" strikes the ear with an antique ring that suggests "old, unhappy, far-off things, and battles long ago." The archaic sound of the term as a synonym for "unbelief" or "free thought" signals the passing of one phase of an enduring conflict between Church and World . . . the infidel is gone.[1]

Marty's book was outdated before it hit the market. The sixties spawned a modern resurgence of atheism which has secularized American society, removing religion not only from the schools but from most public functions of society. It all began in the crazy sixties when I was just beginning high school in New York City.

An Irreligious Education

My high school had a noble history and could claim such famous graduates as the modern composer George Gershwin. The edifice has long since been replaced by Lincoln Center

---

[1]Martin Marty, *The Infidel: Freethought and American Religion* (Cleveland: Meridian Books, 1961), p. 11.

and other buildings, but several memories may never disappear from my mind.

I remember when I found a marijuana cigarette in the pencil holder of my desk. The reefer had been left by a student from the previous class. Drugs were so common they were openly sold in the halls and lunchrooms. Entering a restroom meant breathing enough "grass" to keep you high for a week.

Several teachers extolled the virtues of their own drug experimentation. The administrators simply looked the other way. Since the faculty members were inviting students for pot parties *after* school, the authorities felt they had no grounds for discipline.

Or perhaps the administrators ignored the drug scene because because they were too busy dealing with frequent demonstrations, strikes and bomb threats at the school. The anti-war movement had a firm grip on the "intellectuals" of the faculty and student body. To be anti-American was the "in" thing. Patriotism, rather than being a bold eagle, was a dead duck. America stood for everything that was wrong with the world.

The civil rights movement was also at its height. Radical blacks had organized clubs which fomented trouble in the school. The Black Muslims were highly visible for the first time and they filled the school with racial tension. The liberal white teachers could not understand why the Muslims hated them so much and called them "white devils." After all, these white liberals had worked for black civil rights. They failed to see that these Black Muslims were no respecters of any white person.

Crime also posed a major problem in our school—one of the first high schools in the city with a policeman patrolling each floor. The teachers lived in fear. When the bell rang to signal that class was over, the students filed out and the teacher locked himself inside the room. He did not reopen the door until the bell had rung for the next class to start. Several teachers had been robbed between class periods, and one had been raped.

The only people willing to teach in such an inner-city school either were crazy or had a cause to champion. The faculty therefore was composed largely of loonies who were crazier than the students. Some of them were especially memorable.

My Economics teacher, a Polish Jew who had survived a Nazi concentration camp, liked to pull up her sleeve and show us the number tattooed on her wrist by the Nazis. She did this at least once a week. A committed Marxist, she hated capitalism and the "American dream." She assured us that a "planned economy" by the government would eradicate poverty and inequality. She also frequently attacked religion because it was "a drug which keeps the workers enslaved to the blood-sucking capitalists." Such attacks on religion made my school days interesting.

My Biology teacher, who had been raised in a fundamentalist Christian home, exploited every chance to sermonize on the mistakes in the Bible and the evils of Christianity. To him, evolution was not a theory but a fact which refuted the Bible. During one class he ignited a dish of sulfur so we could see and smell what hell would be like if the fire and brimstone of the Bible were literal. Of course, there followed a discourse on the stupidity and danger of the belief in hell. As is often the case with such people, instead of being simply non-Christian, he was aggressively anti-Christian.

My Chemistry teacher was a hippie who wore the beads and gypsy dresses of her caste and lived in Greenwich Village, which, in those days, was a center of the "flower-power" generation. The biggest nutcase on the faculty, she got high before coming to school and thus did weird things in class: She addressed all her students as "boobies"; threw chalk at them without warning; splashed water at everyone in lab; and, worst of all, pounded her dusty chalk eraser on the pants or skirts of hapless students sitting in the front row. My black pants were a frequent target. Obviously, very little learning took place in her class.

This teacher's attacks on religion focused on its suppression of "natural" urges and desires. Her frequent challenge to her students was, "Why is it wrong to have sex whenever the opportunity presents itself? If it feels good, do it."

My Spanish teacher was a flamboyant, antireligion homosexual who lived the maxim, "If it feels good, do it," by inviting male students to his apartment for "special tutoring." He had worked his way down the roll to the letter "K" when he suffered a nervous breakdown. The entire class cheered when told he would not return. One of his colleagues was overheard saying, " I guess it *is* possible to have too much of a good thing."

My history teacher was also on an antireligion campaign. Even though her tirades rarely had anything to do with our history lesson, she was sure to bring up the horrible deeds of religious people. And though she claimed all religions were guilty of many wicked deeds, because her background was Jewish nearly all her disparaging remarks were aimed at Christianity. She loved to describe in detail the tortures of the Spanish Inquisition. To her, the Middle Ages were the *Dark* Ages.

In one unforgettable history class she launched into a discourse on why she would never be a Christian. One of her reasons: "I could never accept Christianity because it teaches that if a baby is not baptized, it gets roasted in the fires of hell." Though most of her students realized her ignorance of Christianity, only one objected to her misrepresentation. The rest thought her antireligion crusade more interesting than her history lessons.

Most students in this school came from a Christian background and simply ignored the disparaging remarks made by their teachers, but I belonged to the Regents class of students who were expected to be the "intellectuals" of the student body. We had our own lunchroom where we frequently discussed "intellectual issues." One of my friends was Ivan (not his real name), who had been raised an atheist by his Russian immigrant parents. He lived in Greenwich Village, was heavily involved in the drug and sex scene, and was also a leader of the leftist group at the school. Ivan and I were part of a clique which used to talk for hours about politics, drugs, sex, and religion. The teachers liked any student who supported their pet positions, so comments made in class by liberal Regents, such as Ivan, were always received with much appreciation.

No More Apple Pie

Under those circumstances it was only natural that atheism, or at least a good dose of skepticism, was a mark of intellectual respectability. The poem "Invictus," by William Ernest Henley, beckoning us to chart our own destiny without help from any supposed gods or God, was read and studied in several classes. We were taught that a new day was dawning for America and we had to rush to catch up with it. Tomorrow belonged to those brave enough to abandon yesterday. My generation itched to tear down the past and rebuild a better future. This was our hope and our dream.

Martin Marty could not know the sixties would spark this resurgence of unbelief in North America. He wrote his book on infidels in the late fifties when God, country, Mom, and apple pie were still the status quo. In one decade, however, the status quo would swerve to the left.

2

The Erosion of Freedom

By the end of the sixties most state universities had joined the antireligion crusade and were publishing atheistic and skeptical books which attacked religion in general and Christianity in particular. Books attacking the existence of God spewed from the university presses. (Some of these books are listed in the bibliography.) By publishing such books with taxpayers' moneys, public education announced it would no longer be neutral toward religion. Various leaders within public education were launching an unholy crusade against religion.

Enter Madalyn Murray O'Hair

The drive to secularize America, however, actually had begun a few years earlier. The secularists won their first battle when atheist Madalyn Murray O'Hair spearheaded a successful drive to remove prayer and Bible reading from the schools.[1]

Madalyn was and still is the best-known atheist in America. Although she often denied being a Communist (for obvious propaganda reasons), her son William Murray has revealed she was a member of various leftist groups which served

---

[1]William Murray, *My Life Without God* (Nashville: Thomas Nelson, 1982), p. 84.

as fronts for the Communist party; she even chaired the Baltimore chapter of the Communist organization, Fair Play for Cuba.[2] (Lee Harvey Oswald, who assassinated President Kennedy, was a member of the New Orleans chapter of Fair Play for Cuba.)

Madalyn cultivated many relationships with pro-Marxist individuals and groups. When the Communist party opened a bookstore in Baltimore, Madalyn was asked to run it. One of the original lawyers in her case against prayer and Bible reading in the schools was the legal aid for the Communist party. Members of the Communist party frequently met at her house. One of her greatest "thrills" was meeting Gus Hall, leader of the Communist party in America.[3]

At one time O'Hair attempted to emigrate to Russia and even renounced her American citizenship. When she visited the Soviet embassy in Paris to finalize her request for a visa, the officials told her to go back and work for the revolution in America. Madalyn took this advice seriously. Her battle to forbid prayer and Bible reading in the public schools was apparently a direct political consequence of the advice given her by the Soviets. No wonder Judge Pendergast of the Baltimore Superior Court ruled:

> It is abundantly clear that the petitioner's real objective is to drive every concept of religion out of the public school system. If God were removed from the classroom, there would remain only atheism. The word is derived from the Greek *atheos*, meaning "without a god." Thus the beliefs of virtually all the pupils would be subordinated to those of Madalyn Murray.[4]

The Courtship of Madalyn

Once O'Hair could thwart the will of the people and criminalize historic practices such as school prayer, she and her leftist and radical friends possessed the key to destroying the role of religion in American life: Let the courts do the dirty

---

[2]Ibid., pp. 21f.
[3]Ibid., pp. 21–84.
[4]Ibid., p. 72.

work of destroying religion in America.

Infidels have never been able to persuade the common man that there is no God. Therefore their only recourse has been to use the courts to punish believers by denying them the freedom to practice and propagate their religion.

History has shown that if religion is allowed the freedoms of speech, assembly and the press, it cannot be destroyed. Unbelief, however, cannot successfully compete in the open marketplace of ideas. It can thrive only where belief may not express itself. The repression of religion in the Soviet Union exemplifies this; there atheism prevails only because it is forced upon the people. Ironically, the underground church in the U.S.S.R. thrives in spite of legal persecution.

When Madalyn returned to the U.S., determined to remove religion from American society, the Soviet system of suppressing religion no doubt showed her the way. The Soviets, through the courts, had criminalized any public expression of religion, except at a time and place sanctioned by the state. Even the home did not have religious freedom—teaching one's children to believe in God was a crime. Religion could not be allowed any freedom because, if unfettered, it would win more people than unbelief.[5]

The religious leaders of America did not realize, until too late, that war had been declared on them. Antireligion laws and policies already had been passed before the religious world woke up to find its privileged status in society gone and its political and religious freedoms severely curtailed. They had slept through the war and now faced an uphill battle to regain even some of the ground they had lost. But history has repeatedly shown that once a freedom is lost, it is almost impossible to regain.

Religion Gets Kicked Out of School

The last twenty years have witnessed many attempts by religious leaders to repeal those laws which deny the freedom

---

[5]G. Kline, *Religious and Anti-religious Thought in Russia* (Chicago: University of Chicago Press, 1968).

of religious expression in public life, but these leaders have not gained one significant victory. Prayer has not been returned to the schools, and the courts have even ruled against the displaying of the Ten Commandments in public schools. Recent court rulings have removed the prayer at baccalaureate services. A public school principle demanded a picture of a school club (that used the Bible for devotional exercises) be excised from the yearbook. Such political acts of suppression reveal that the drive to secularize American society has continued full steam ahead.

The irrational nature of the infidels' fear of religion is seen in the courts' rulings against giving students a minute of silence—lest a student pray. To deny people the right of a moment of silence reveals the hostility of antireligion judges against the free expression of religion in public life.

This situation is unique in American history because people previously assumed the state would follow the will of the majority of the people. While the vast majority of the populace is at least moderately religious, government policies are becoming more antireligious than ever. That the vast majority of the population wants prayer returned to the schools is ignored by the Supreme Court. Social-activist justices are forcing their views on the nation by arbitrary law.

Eugene Methvin, senior editor of the popular *Reader's Digest*, insists the courts, particularly the Supreme Court, have been on an antireligion campaign:

> Eight Justices in 1962–63 rulings decided that this [amendment] meant public-school students cannot voluntarily pray together or listen to a Bible reading. At that time, constitutional scholars overwhelmingly agreed with Harvard Law Dean (and later U.S. Solicitor General) Erwin Griswold that these decisions were "sheer invention" without historical or constitutional grounding. Polls have shown that Americans—four or five to one—favor a constitutional amendment, if necessary, to reverse the Justices' policies.
>
> Yet, for two decades the Court presided over a virtual all-out war on religion by a militant minority of atheists and civil libertarians with federal judges as their enforcers. Judges have told youngsters they cannot sit together at their lunch hour and read their Bibles. With the federal judiciary as their guide,

school authorities told a handicapped girl in El Paso, Texas, not to use her rosary on a school bus. In Minnesota, high school students were allowed to write on such topics as demon possession and suicide notes—but not on the Resurrection of Christ. Four years ago, five Justices declared unconstitutional the Kentucky legislature's decision to post the Ten Commandments in public school classrooms.[6]

Government of the Courts, by the Courts, and for the Courts

The antireligion stance of the courts would be understandable if they represented the wishes of the majority of the people. But now we have a situation where the desires of the majority are ignored and a small, elite group of secularists are making antireligion policies at will. Thus, today, instead of the infidel being persecuted, the believer is singled out for persecution. His freedom of expression is curtailed. His right of free assembly is denied. And even his freedom of the press and of the media is threatened. This has never before happened in a free nation where elected officials are supposed to administer the will of the people. Governmental policies in America are supposed to be "of the people, by the people, and for the people." Obviously, something has gone wrong with the American way of government.

We live in an age of arbitrary law, in which the courts ignore the Constitution, legal precedent, and the will of the people. Instead of Congress enacting laws, as stipulated by the Constitution, the courts make laws. The judges have robbed the American people of their right to rule themselves.

Since the Federal and Supreme Court judges are not elected but appointed, the people of this country have virtually no means of removing them. And because they are appointed to their offices for life, the only hope people have is that these "lawmakers" retire or die.

These judges bear an ominous burden of guilt, not only for strangling the religious freedom of the American people but also for legalizing the slaughter of millions of innocent

---

[6]Eugene Methvin, "The Supreme Court: Justice in the Balance," *Reader's Digest* (Nov., 1985), pp. 100–101.

children, cruelly murdered under the guise of "therapeutic" contraceptive abortion. These infidel judges will be held accountable for legalized murder and will stand condemned before the judgment of history and the Judgment of God on the last day. Their acts bear the same inhumanity as those of Nazi judges who signed orders sending millions of innocent people to an inhuman death in concentration camps. There is little difference between the agonizing deaths inflicted on the unborn in abortion clinics and the Jews in Hitler's death camps.

Unbelief by Any Other Name . . .

Now, unbelief goes by many names: atheism, rationalism, skepticism, freethinking, deism, liberalism, humanism, materialism, Marxism, communism, socialism or even secular humanism. In recent years secular humanists have been getting exposure in the media because they have made themselves highly visible. They are organized and have their own official creed and publications. They do not "pussy-foot" around by pretending to be anything else than an organization of infidels, dedicated to forcing their atheistic philosophy on American society.

The secular humanists have copied the Church's methods. Just as Christians produce books, pamphlets and films which promote their biblical message, the secular humanists exploit mass media to promote the suppression of religion and the secularization of America—much as the secular state of the Soviet Union. Just as Christians hold seminars and evangelistic crusades, the humanists hold their seminars and rallies. Just as believers focus great attention on college students because many can be converted, the various atheistic societies almost entirely aim their efforts toward student populations.

Believers and infidels on college and university campuses differ, however, in one area: tolerance. The infidels pressure state college administrators to run believers off the campus. They want bans against Bible studies in the dorms and any other religious meetings on the campus. But when do we hear of Christian students on state college campuses demanding that atheists be barred?

One state university's administration decided to forbid distribution of religious literature on the campus; they made it a crime to give a Bible to a fellow student! The Supreme Court recently upheld this suppression of the freedoms of speech, press and religion for Christian students. What makes all this absurd is that the administration had no objections to atheists meeting in the classroom, or passing out any literature they desired!

Too many other examples come to mind. A student was told he could not bring his Bible to school to read during lunch or study time. A group of students who met at lunchtime to read and discuss the Bible and pray together were ordered to stop the practice. A girl who gave out Christmas cards with a religious theme was suspended from her high school. Two teenage boys who witnessed to their fellow students and passed out tracts were suspended from school. A group of teachers who met before school to pray for wisdom for the day were told to stop or be fired. A community college which would not allow students to meet for Bible study featured X-rated films in the student union and sponsored courses in witchcraft. A teacher, charged with reverently speaking of "God" before her students, was disciplined. When she asked if she was permitted to use the word "God" before her students, she was told it could be used only in blasphemy or cursing, but never in reverence! At the same school an atheist teacher had complete freedom to preach his unbelief to students. Evidently "academic freedom" and "freedom of speech" applied only to the unbeliever.

The courts' condoning of such actions perverts the purpose of the U.S. Constitution, for while the Soviet constitution espouses the doctrine of "the separation of Church and State," this concept is absent from the U.S. Constitution. Sad to say, the average American does not know this.[7] The American

---

[7]*Biblical Principles Concerning Issues of Importance to Godly Christians* (Plymouth, Mass.: Plymouth Rock Foundation, 1984), pp. 196–211.

forefathers wrote the First Amendment to protect religion from the control or persecution of the state. In other words, the Constitution was designed to tie the hands of the government. Thus the First Amendment says the state ". . . shall make no law respecting an establishment of religion, or prohibiting the free exercise thereof. . . ." Yet, infidel judges now interpret the First Amendment to mean that the hands of religion should be tied, that the state should prohibit the free public expression of religion, and control or persecute religion. In effect, the Constitution has been made to stand on its head.

This is the exact purpose of the infidel, as Madalyn Murray O'Hair has said, "I want to be able to walk down any street in America and not see a cross or any other sign of religion."[8] The very idea that religious groups should not be allowed to identify themselves publicly by the display of their symbols, such as a cross, star of David, or star and crescent, should be viewed as a clear example of the infidel's desire to deny people the freedom of expressing their religion.

When we seek out the source of this modern atheistic militancy in America, we find much of it is carried on with evangelistic zeal by a small tight-knit group of atheists who promote their cause through Arno Press and Prometheus Press as their main publishing houses. They produce periodicals under a dozen or so names—which change frequently. *Free Inquiry* and *The American Rationalist* are two current examples of such periodicals. Examination of the names listed as the editors reveals the same people are behind several of these publications.

Although dozens of atheistic organizations exist in the U.S., and though Madalyn O'Hair is still the leading cult figure of popular atheism in this country, if any individual may be considered the guiding intellect of the movement, the honor (if any) must go to Paul Kurtz. *Science Digest* featured Kurtz and his antireligion crusade in an article entitled "The #1 Skeptic and His Debunking Brigade" (Spring Special, 1980). Kurtz and

---

[8]Murray, ibid., p. 98.

an associate, Gordon Stein, take turns being editor and associate editor of the various atheistic publications which their movement sponsors from its headquarters in Buffalo, New York.

This small group of evangelistic atheists wields astounding influence, especially when one considers the minimal circulation of its publications. One of its main periodicals, *Free Inquiry,* reportedly has only around twelve thousand subscribers. (In comparison, even the mundane *Weed Journal* has over thirty thousand subscribers!) In addition, the movement's books are unavailable in most bookstores. The group has great difficulty keeping its periodicals and journals financially afloat. Yet, its atheistic ideas and agenda of secularization have a stranglehold on American educational and legal institutions.

Obviously, the influence of the various atheistic groups grossly exceeds their numbers. Why? They make up in zeal for their lack in numbers because they are committed to an unholy crusade: to destroy belief in God and terminate all religious organizations. The consuming desire of modern atheists is summed up by infidel Paul Blanshard in three words: "a secular state."[9] That is the goal for which they fight.

---

[9] Paul Blanshard, ed., *Classics of Free Thought* (Buffalo: Prometheus Books, 1977).

3

The New Atheism

Militancy is the difference between what was historically known as "atheism" and the modern movement of "anti-theism." The atheists of the old school took a rather relaxed, passive attitude toward God and the Bible. They felt that if people were foolish enough to believe in religion, that was their problem. These atheists did not feel the need to read through the Bible, desperately seeking contradictions or errors. They did not sit up night after night feverishly trying to formulate attacks against religion. They simply ignored religion.

Hating a Nonexistent God

The situation abruptly changed after Hegel (1770–1831). Atheists became anti-theists as they were now actively "against" God, seeking to wage war on God and on those who believed in Him. Thus the pure atheism of nonbelief gave way to a crusade of anti-theism. No longer did they simply not believe in God. They now *hated* God and wished to destroy all faith, love and obedience directed to Him.

Hegel and those who followed him, such as Feuerbach, Neitszche, Marx, etc., believed that God had to be pushed aside in order for man to be free to be his own god. The only way for man to ascend the throne of divinity was for God to step down. It was not simply that God did not exist; God *must* not and *ought* not exist.[1]

Thus modern atheists deny God's existence because they actually hate God. They hate Him because this God demands they serve Him and fulfill the destiny He has decreed for them. This God gives man a revealed law which dictates what is right and wrong. God thus robs man of the freedom of being and choosing whatever he wants. God is viewed as the enemy that must be destroyed in order for man to reach his full potential. Instead of God being the measure of all things, man must be the measure of all things.

The only way atheists can strike a blow directly against God is to deny His existence. Is it any wonder then that the modern anti-theists' champion is Prometheus who said, "I hate all the gods," who said he would rather suffer death than be the servant of the gods. Prometheus did not deny that the gods existed. His was the rebel cry, "I will not serve you. I will not acknowledge your authority over me. I deny your very existence, for I will not bow down to you."

Prometheus' hatred of God and all He stands for is the soul and substance of modern anti-theism. This is why the name "Prometheus Books" was chosen for the major publisher of infidel literature. The truth of this observation is obvious because only a strong emotional antipathy toward God could fuel the zeal and enthusiasm of Paul Kurtz and his unholy crusade.

On one of my radio programs, I debated George Smith who wrote a book entitled *The Case Against God*. During our debate it became apparent that Mr. Smith was not simply an atheist, but was rather a typical modern anti-theist who saw God as his enemy. He reminded me of Madalyn O'Hair who would at times go outside during a thunderstorm and dare God to strike her dead as she shook her fists at Him.

Modern anti-theists use atheism as the ultimate means of attacking God. They raise their fist to heaven and say, "I will

---

[1] For an excellent modern analysis of the anti-theism of Hegel and those who followed him, see Vincent P. Miceli, *The Gods of Atheism* (Harrison, N.Y.: Roman Catholic Books, 1971).

deny your existence because this is the ultimate way I have of attacking you." Modern anti-theism has thus become a way to get back at God. It is an attempt to slap God in the face.

Anyone who reads its literature or debates its leaders finds that modern Anti-theism is fueled by such ignoble motives as bitterness, rage, and hatred. Its spokesmen manifest an angry spirit which rages first against God and then (because they cannot confront God directly) against those who dare believe in Him.

This irrational rage motivates some of them to read the Bible, frantically searching for ways to attack it. Obsessed with the need to debunk the Bible, they cannot rest until they have rooted out all faith in the Bible as God's Word. Modern anti-theists are on a crusade against the Bible as well as God.

One clear example of the anti-Christian bias of modern anti-theists is the monthly newsletter called *The Bible Errancy*. While its editor claims to be objective and scholarly in his investigation of the truthfulness of the Bible, in his April 16, 1984 (Issue 16) edition he let the proverbial cat out of the bag: He had requested Madalyn O'Hair to allow him booth space at her atheist convention in Kentucky, but she refused because, "The Bible needs to be thrown in the trash. . . . We instituted an extensive educational program to wean atheists away, as fast as we can, from . . . a return to the Bible" (p.3).

Obviously, Madalyn does not want anyone, including an atheist, to read the Bible, and the editor's response to Madalyn revealed his attitude toward the Bible was the same as hers. The motivation behind his newsletter was to get people to "throw the Bible in the trash." He would do whatever was necessary to undermine the trustworthiness of the Bible.

With such an irrational hatred of the Bible as the motivation behind *The Bible Errancy*, it is no surprise to find the newsletter filled with every logical, historical and biblical error known to man. Apparently, the editor superficially rushes through the Bible looking for anything he can twist into a contradiction or error. Of course, he does not indicate he has ever had any education in the original languages or the text and history of the Bible.

Atheism by Decree

As stated in the previous chapter, modern anti-theism's crusade against God and the Bible faces a giant hurdle: History has shown that people will remain religious despite so-called rational or scientific arguments against God's existence. Abstract philosophical arguments have little meaning for the average person because the existence of God has always been, for most people, a matter of common sense. Thus when atheism competes with theism in the open marketplace of ideas, it never convinces the average people who make up the bulk of the population.

Since their abstract philosophical arguments have never secularized a nation, anti-theists have in the end used force to suppress religion. Thus in Communist lands, while Marx taught that religion will fade away in the light of the glories of atheism, communist leaders tacitly acknowledge today that Marx's doctrine (on this point) does not work. Religion will not disappear by itself. Left to itself, religion will always grow. One must force people to give up their religion.

What the atheists have done in Russia, Cuba, China, etc. provides a graphic lesson in what happens when the infidel is in control. The social and political implications must not be ignored, because the anti-theists in the West call for the same suppression of religion which the Communists use in their lands.

First, the courts remove all religion from public life. No public religious ceremonies can be allowed. Religion must be rooted out of the public schools, and church schools must be destroyed. All hospitals, colleges, camps, orphanages, youth organizations, etc., which are run by religious groups must be taken over by the state which then removes religion from them. No religion can be allowed to broadcast over radio or TV. No publications can be allowed. No street preaching or home Bible studies can be permitted. Converting children or anyone to your religion is made a crime. Even the singing of Christmas carols must be forbidden.

We can say many things about the Communists, but we

cannot say they are stupid. They know that if religion is allowed freedom of expression, the vast majority of people will be religious. Unbelief will always lose out in the end. The religious nature of man cannot be supressed as long as man is man.[2]

Second, the government applies direct pressure to the populace because even after the courts make laws against religion, the people will keep right on believing. The basic necessities of life must be denied those who continue to believe. Religious leaders must be either killed or placed in slave camps. Church buildings must be either destroyed or used as anti-religion museums and warehouses. Seminaries must be shut down to prevent the education of future religious leaders. Young people must be denied higher education and better careers if they are believers. The children of believers must be taken into the state's custody and sent to atheistic state homes.

If believers were denied the basic necessities of life, higher education, better jobs, the custody of their own children, and if they were persecuted even to death for their faith, it was assumed by Communist leaders that believers would give up their religion in order to escape persecution. Those leaders now realize that even such harsh persecution has not destroyed the faith of their enslaved peoples.[3]

In fact, there are actually *more* evangelical Christians in the atheistic Soviet Union, China, Cuba, etc., than before the people were enslaved by their Marxist dictators. The Catholic church is stronger in such places as Poland than ever before in their history. Islam continues to grow even in the Soviet Union. The moment that China relaxed its persecution of religion, the temples and churches filled to overflowing. In every instance where unbelief is the policy of the state, and religion is severely persecuted, the people have never given up their

---

[2]For a modern statement on the religious nature of man, see: Vernon Reynolds and Ralph E. Tanner, *The Biology of Religion* (White Plains: Longman, 1983).

[3]On the failure of atheism in the Soviet Union, see: Oxana Antic, "How The Soviet Union Promotes Atheism: An Empire Aligned Against God," *Liberty*, Jan./Feb. 1985, pp. 17–19.

religion, although they may have had to go underground with their faith.

State persecution of believers may actually *increase* the number of believers. In China, after the communes were set up, the order was given to count the Christians in each commune. If there was more than one believer in a commune, the other Christians were distributed to communes which had no Christians—under the assumption that if believers were separated from each other, they would eventually lose heart and give up their faith. But the opposite occurred.

Christians were scattered throughout China at government expense, and were sent even into sections of China which had never had a Christian witness. In effect, the government placed one Christian missionary in every commune! As a result, all of China was evangelized and there are now more Christians than ever before. Entire communes have become Christian. The government cannot possibly root out all the house churches that make up today's underground church in China.

The Politics of Atheism

"But," someone may ask, "what does all this have to do with the various atheistic groups in America? Are you trying to say they are all Communists?" As a matter of record, many atheists who have gone public with their campaign to secularize America do not hesitate to admit they are Communists, leftists or socialists, and that their anti-religion activity is an outgrowth of their political commitment to Hegel or Marx. It is thus no surprise to find that most of the modern movements which espouse atheism do so as a necessary ingredient of their leftist ideologies. Modern anti-theists proclaim their unbelief in God as part of a "package deal" which includes totalitarian socialism as the ultimate goal.

Of course, a few atheists would deny that their atheism is connected with socialism or communism. Upon closer questioning, however, these individuals virtually always have a hidden political agenda that includes the denial of religious freedom. But while there may be somewhere a few patriotic atheists who are capitalists and proud of it (although I have yet to meet such a person), our main concern should be with the various organizations and leaders who make up the modern movement of anti-theism.

This movement should not be viewed as a sophomoric, philosophical discussion of the proofs for the existence of God. Its adherents have a political agenda that calls for the suppression of all religious freedom. Thus this is not a philosophic game which is to be played by philosophers in their ivory towers. The ultimate issues deal with the future of religious liberty.

Once we discover that today's atheistic movements in the U.S. have the same political agenda as do their counterparts in Communist countries, we realize that unbelief is not just a philosophical debate about abstract arguments for and against God's existence. The fundamental issue today is not philosophy but political science. And, we must add, the worse mistake most believers make about modern atheism is made at this point.

Some believers have naively assumed that modern atheistic attacks on religion are made by sincere people honestly searching for the truth. They mistakenly believe that if they answer these anti-theists with equal sincerity, these infidels will come to the faith. Yet, if history teaches anything, it teaches that answering professional skeptics is a never-ending task. As soon as one argument is answered, the infidel simply pulls another one out of his hat.

It requires little intelligence, however, to contrive groundless theories to attack something. The trick is to deny having to prove the theory. Arguments from silence are always the easiest method in this kind of deception. And, as shown below, the atheists use arguments based on silence for most of their attacks on the Bible.

Consider, for example, the Mosaic authorship of the Pentateuch. When Jean Astruc, an apostate Jew, initiated the attack on the morality of the Ten Commandments, he saw that the best way to destroy it was to deny its historicity. He did this by claiming Moses did not actually write it. First came the declaration that Moses never existed. When the absurdity of this objection became obvious to all, infidels countered that there had been no writing in the days of Moses. When scholars demonstrated that writing existed *before* Moses' day, they argued that the style of writing found in the Pentateuch did not exist in Moses' day. When defenders showed this argument invalid, the attackers continued an endless succession of speculative arguments.[4] As soon as one argument was refuted, the infidels simply conjured a new theory. At no point did they ever acknowledge that the previous arguments had been answered, because the real issue was not Mosaic authorship but the absolute morality of God's law.

Nearly all the critical attacks on the historicity of Moses have been arguments from silence. It was assumed that the lack of evidence for writing in Moses' day proved writing did not exist. The fact that such evidence was awaiting discovery reveals the absurdity of the infidel's tactic of arguing from silence. The only logical deduction these infidels could legitimately have made was that *at that time* no evidence existed for writing in Moses' day. To go beyond this and state there was no writing in Moses' day was a logical fallacy. One can deduce only silence from silence. However, at least ninety percent of the critical attacks on Scripture are based on the false assumption that one can validly argue from silence.

This logical error frequently creeps into debates with modern infidels, as shown on a radio program I hosted in Chicago for several years. Each month I spent ninty minutes interviewing and debating skeptics, atheists, cultists, occultists, and religious quacks. Listeners found the format quite exciting because they could hear live debates between a believer and an infidel.

On several programs I debated well-known atheists, but a debate with one typical, dogmatic atheist in 1983 remains etched on my memory. She argued almost exclusively from silence. She dogmatically stated that Nazareth did not exist in

---

[4]For a review of the history of critical attacks on Moses, see: Oswald Allis, *The Five Books of Moses* (Phillipsburg, N.J.: Presbyterian and Reformed Pub. Co., 1964) and Josh McDowell, *More Evidence That Demands a Verdict* (San Bernardino, Calif.: Campus Crusade, 1975).

the first century. What was her proof? The village of Nazareth is not mentioned by Josephus or the Talmud! She also claimed the Apostle Paul did not believe in the virgin birth of Christ. Her proof? He nowhere mentions it in his epistles! A transcript of the debate, given in a later chapter, provides an example of how most modern infidels argue against the Bible and religion.

Amid such debate, the worst mistake that can be made is to treat the modern atheistic arguments in an abstract philosophical manner. The arguments are given, not in the interests of finding the truth but as part of a political agenda for the secularization of American society and the destruction of religious freedom, a fulfillment of atheists' socialist views. Many people are incredulous at such a claim, so we need to look carefully at the roots of modern atheism.

Historically, the modern-day atheistic movement follows in the steps of Robert Owen, the socialist labor leader of the last century who led the last great movement of unbelief in England and the U.S. Owen was quite candid about what he opposed and why he opposed it. His platform was threefold. He was against (1) private ownership of property, (2) the nuclear family, and (3) religion, because it is the source of the first two concepts.

This socialism, known as "Owenism," mandated atheism as a necessary step to overturn private ownership and destroy the family unit. Owen's commitment to the absolute supremacy of the state required the destruction of any authority which claimed to be independent from or higher than the state. Thus religion had to go because it denied the supremacy of the state in all things. Owen actually had adopted anti-theism rather than just atheism.[5]

The Myth of Academic Freedom

What about the modern infidel organizations and publications? Do they, in the spirit of Owenism, treat religion as

---

[5]For a complete discussion of Robert Owen and his political atheism, see: Susan Budd, *Varieties of Unbelief* (New York: Holmes & Meier Pubs., 1977).

an abstract philosophical issue or do they wish to force their unbelief upon the nation and suppress the freedom of religious expression? Perhaps this question is best answered by observing the attitude infidel organizations have toward allowing creationists to present their position to students in high school or college. This issue is quite simple and it reveals the true attitude modern atheists have toward the freedom of speech for religious people.

Here is the issue at stake: Should creationists be allowed equal time to state their case so students can make an informed, intelligent choice? Should creation scientists be given the freedom to express their views? Should public debates be allowed between evolutionists and creationists?

Now, if the creationists' arguments are as stupid and devoid of scientific merit as the evolutionists claim, the smartest way to discredit creation science is to let it be heard. No one will believe it if the theory is as absurd as the infidel scientists claim. What is there to fear?

Also, shouldn't students be allowed to hear all sides of an issue, even if the present administration takes only one side? After all, "academic freedom" in the U.S. allows a Communist to teach a course on why America is the cause of all the evil in the world and why the Soviet Union is the working man's paradise. Marcus, Angela Davis, and a host of other leftists have done exactly this for years in state universities.

In addition, censorship certainly should not be practiced on the university or college campus. All ideas should be expressed freely. We should not go back to the Dark Ages when no one was permitted to question the "orthodox" view, or suggest an alternative view. Modern liberal education has always prided itself on the student's right to question the position of the teacher. Let all ideas compete freely in the marketplace of education.

The above tenets are championed when atheists and other unbelievers desire the right to attack religion and teach their own world view, but once they have gained the right to air their ideas in the name of academic freedom, they have no intention of allowing creationists the same freedom to state their case. Creation scientists are to be censored. There is no academic freedom for them.[6]

The average atheist sees no contradiction in his hypocritical attitude that demands academic freedom for himself but denies it to believers. For example, in one state college an atheist is always appointed to teach the religion course. The administrators claim that if a believer taught it, the course would be biased. When someone suggested, however, that a theist should be allowed to teach an "unbiased" course on atheism, the hoots and howls could be heard all the way to Moscow. The atheists would not extend to believers the same freedoms they claim for themselves.

Many evolutionist professors will not allow creation scientists to speak because the professors have misrepresented creationists as stupid, lacking intelligent spokesmen or arguments. If the creationists received freedom to speak, the students would discover that creation scientists hold Ph.D.'s as do the evolutionists and are capable of presenting intelligent arguments and scientific evidence for their position. The typical atheistic professor is attached to the theory of evolution for political and ethical reasons and will recoil in horror at the thought of their students hearing the creationist position.

When Aldous Huxley, author of *Brave New World*, was asked on TV why his generation leaped to accept the theory of evolution, he was honest enough to admit they adopted evolution because they wanted to be rid of the moral restraints of religion.[7] They accepted evolution for moral reasons, not scientific reasons. This emotional attachment to the theory of evolution makes it difficult for evolutionists to have any scientifically based discussion of the subject. For them, evolution *has* to be true. The moral implications of creation would be too dreadful to bear.

---

[6]For an update, see: *Liberty*, Jan./Feb. 1985, pp. 4–9. For details on legal problems contact: The Creation Research Society, 2717 Cranbrook Rd., Ann Arbor, Michigan 48104.

[7]Quoted in the sermon, "Maker of Heaven and Earth," preached by Dr. James Kennedy (Coral Ridge Presbyterian Church, Coral Ridge, Fla.), January 22, 1984.

In my many encounters with atheists, skeptics, freethinkers, and the like, I have yet to meet one who does not feel "there ought to be a law" to curb religion's freedom of public expression. They all seem to agree with O'Hair that the courts should ban prayer in the schools; restrict any public religious ceremonies or display of symbols; dismantle the system of military chaplains; revoke the tax-exempt status of church buildings; obliterate "In God we trust" from U.S. currency; and delete "One nation under God" from the Pledge of Allegiance.

Many of these atheists make it abundantly clear they even want the evangelistic outreach of believers banned. And they are succeeding. For example, it is now illegal in New York City and other large cities to hand out religious literature in public parks or on public beaches; it is illegal to preach on any public property. In some cities such as Atlanta, Georgia, it is now illegal to hold a Bible study or prayer meeting in a private home without permission from the city. Clearly, the day of religious freedom in America has passed. Believers must wake up to this while they still have time to recoup their losses. The longer they remain inactive, the harder it will be to regain their civil rights.

The restrictions modern infidels wish to place on religious expression would ultimately confine religion to one's private thoughts. No expression of those thoughts would be permitted, whether in the home or in society at large. Of course, people always will be free to think what they want because the state will never devise a way to monitor or control the ideas in their minds. But such freedom is a ruse. Giving people freedom to think what they want while denying them freedom to express those thoughts is the soul and substance of tyranny.

But what about the philosophical arguments? Don't we have to deal with them, even if they are politically motivated? Of course we must deal with the attempts of unbelievers to undermine the Faith. But while doing this we must remember that refuting the present popular arguments will only lead to the infidels thinking up some new ones.

The task of refutation is endless because the arguments are morally and politically motivated. Even when his arguments are shown to be false, the infidel will not believe because he doesn't *want* to believe. He is against God not because he *has* to be, but because he *chooses* to be. Even in His own day, Jesus said of such people, "You refuse to come to me to have life" (John 5:40).

4

Defining Atheism

Surveys have shown that the average person considers an "atheist" someone who denies the existence of God; he refuses to believe any god or gods of any shape or form existed in the past, exist now, or will exist in the future. "Atheism," in this popular sense, is a simple, flat denial of the existence of God.

When seeking to understand modern atheism, or anti-theism, however, we encounter a problem: The popular meaning of "atheism" does not fit. Therefore, to surmount this problem, we must follow the rules we normally use when attempting to define any word.

The etymology of "atheism" is found in the combination of two Greek words, *a* + *theos*, which literally means "no god." The term was first used to describe those who denied the existence of the gods of Greece or Rome. In this sense, the early Christians were legally tried and convicted of "atheism" because they believed only in the biblical God and claimed that the gods of the pagan religions did not really exist.

After Western culture was Christianized, "atheism" came to mean a denial of the Christian concept of God as the invisible, self-existent, all-powerful and all-knowing triune Being who is the Creator of the universe and the Savior of mankind. Atheism as a philosophical position, however, did not appear until the Renaissance. During this "Age of Reason," which the Rationalists called "The Age of Enlightenment," various thinkers proposed that they could satisfactorily explain man and the world without the need for the concept of God.

Man had now come of age and no longer needed God or His revelation given in the Bible. The universe was one vast machine which functioned according to the dictates of "natural law," so man had no further need for the idea of God. Infidel thinkers declared the universe to be a "closed" system in which there was no room for God. Materialism and empiricism had redefined reality in such a way that the existence and nature of God were excluded from any serious discussion. People were not able to logically disprove the existence of God; they simply defined Him out of existence. Thus the issue was no longer open for debate.

At first, belief in God was viewed as so much superstition. Surely science and education would lead mankind to jettison such a primitive concept. Anything which did not conform to a rationalist's system of logic or was not confirmed by his experience was redefined as myth.

Out of materialism came Nazism on the right and Marxism on the left, and a new stage in the development of atheism began. God was no longer viewed as a harmless relic of the Dark Ages. The concepts of God and belief in Him were now vilified as the origin of all of man's ills.

To such thinkers as Nietzsche, the traditional moral attributes of God (e.g. kindness, mercy and love) were the source of all decadent "slave ethics." Nietzsche turned ethics upside down by calling greed and violence "good" and kindness and mercy "evil." Man therefore could not be free until he shed himself of the concept of God as a snake shedding his skin. Thus, when Nietzsche said, "God is dead," he meant that the concept of God and belief in Him were no longer possible or desirable.

Marx blamed belief in God as the power that held back the Hegelian dialectical process in which society would move from a capitalist to a communist economy. Religion in its simplest form is belief in God and Marx insisted this belief restrained people from creating the classless society. Therefore religion had to be destroyed out of political necessity.

Freud maligned belief in God as a mental illness. He dogmatically taught that anyone who believes in God must have some deep-rooted psychological problem. Man does not need God or His morality. Man will never be "healthy" until he gives up all religious concepts.

Modern anti-theists, as we can see, do not view the existence of God as a harmless philosophical question which may be discussed if there is nothing else better to do. To them, God *cannot* exist because He *must* not exist. The average person finds this all quite confusing. If an atheist does not want to believe in God, that is his right. But if he doesn't believe in God, why does he spend so much time fighting God?

The matter makes no sense unless the atheist objects to God because God is in the way of some goal he has in mind. In other words, the atheist must answer *why* he must deny God. What is the *purpose* of his denial? *What* does he hope to accomplish by attacking faith in God? What *motivates* his crusade against God?

To eliminate this confusion we must define the meaning of "atheism." This will be done in three stages in order to make our definition as accurate as possible. These three steps will cover general reference works, philosophical reference works, and books on atheism.

General Reference Works

When an average person seeks the definition of a word, he will turn to the standard reference works that were part of his education. The source will usually be his dictionary. *Webster's New World Dictionary of the American Language*, for example, defines "atheism" as "the belief that there is no God, or denial that God or gods exist." In the entry for "atheist," it says "an atheist rejects all religious belief and denies the existence of God" (p. 87). If that person wants to dig a little deeper, he will check any encyclopedias he is likely to own. The following excerpts are examples of what he would find.

Collier's Encyclopedia: "Those who explicitly deny the existence of God, by virtue of some metaphysics whose key idea positively excludes Him" (Vol. I, p. 141).

Encyclopedia Americana: "the denial that there is any being or power deserving the name of God or the reverence according God" (p. 604).

Encyclopedia Britannica: "(1) as a denial that there is one supreme object of reverence; (2) as a denial that this object of reverence is also the all-inclusive reality; (3) as a denial that there is any one all-inclusive reality at all; (4) as a denial that the power which rules the world is worthy of our trust; (5) as a denial that this power is a Being with whom we may hold personal communion" (Vol. II, p. 600).

Funk and Wagnall's New Encyclopedia: "atheism . . . denies the existence of deity" (Vol. I, p. 411).

The above reference works are in complete agreement that atheism is the belief that God or gods do not exist, that it is rooted in its own metaphysical system of belief in which God is excluded.

Philosophical Reference Works

Although the average person will end his search at this point because he is now satisfied that he understands the meaning of atheism, some people will want to delve deeper than the standard reference works. They may make a special trip to a local library to consult the reference works that specialize in philosophy. This constitutes the second stage of our research into the meaning of "atheism," and following are examples of statements from philosophical reference works.

The Dictionary of Philosophy (Dagobert D. Runes, ed.) indicates, "Two uses of the term: (a) The Belief that there is no God. (b) Some philosophers have been called "atheistic" because they have not held to a belief in a personal God. Atheism in this sense means 'not theistic' " (p. 26).

The Encyclopedia of Philosophy (Paul Edwards, ed.) acknowledges that much confusion surrounds the definition of atheism. So many peculiar definitions have been made by various modern atheists that "no definition of 'atheism' could hope to be in accord with all the uses of this term" (Vol. I, p. 175).

Yet, according to the author of the article, this does not mean a general definition is impossible. He insists if we adopt the meaning used by the great philosophers throughout the history of philosophy, we can arrive at a clear idea of the meaning of atheism. "According to the most usual definition, an atheist is a person who maintains that there is no God, that is, that the sentence 'God exists' expresses a false proposition . . . a person who rejects belief in God" (Vol. I, p. 175).

Philosophy of Religion (John Hick) is a standard textbook used in many colleges and universities. He defines atheism as "the belief that there is no God of any kind" (p. 4).

A survey of the reference literature on the subject reveals that the standard philosophical reference works give the same basic definition of atheism: the belief that God or gods have never existed, are not existing now and shall never exist in the future anywhere in the universe. But does this agreement prove the standard definition is correct? Perhaps we ought to dig a little deeper yet by examining books specifically written on atheism to see how they define the word. This would be our third stage of investigation.

Books on Atheism

Madalyn Murray O'Hair went to great lengths to define atheism on a number of radio programs. Those definitions were later published in book form under the title, *What on Earth Is an Atheist?*. In the chapter entitled "Definition of Atheism," she states, "I am an atheist and this means at least: I do not believe there is a god, or any gods, personal or in nature, or manifesting himself, herself, or itself in any way" (p. 38).

Lest atheism be accused of being only a negative assertion, she further stated that atheism also encompasses a number of additional beliefs. Thus atheism is *for* certain beliefs as well as being *against* certain beliefs, such as belief in God. She asserts:

> We need a decent, modern, sophisticated and workable set of standards by which we can get along with ourselves and with others (p. 39).
>
> We atheists . . . try to find some basis of rational thinking on which we can base our actions and our beliefs, and we

have it. . . . We accept the technical philosophy of materialism. It is valid philosophy which cannot be discredited. Essentially, materialism's philosophy holds that nothing exists
but natural phenomena. . . . Materialism is a philosophy of
life and living according to rational processes with intellectual
and other capabilities of the individual to be developed to the
highest degree in a social system where this may be possible. . . . There are no supernatural forces, no supernatural
entities such as gods, or heavens, or hells, or life after death.
There are no supernatural forces, nor can there be.

We atheists believe that nature simply exists. Matter is.
Material is (pp. 40–43).

O'Hair's definition shows that the denial of the existence
of God does not take place in a theoretical vacuum. It is the
prior commitment to a world view that excludes God from
the universe. If the atheist's "reality" is reduced to material
objects which can be weighed and measured, then any invisible deities or spirits are an impossibility.

Atheism is positive as well as negative. On the positive
side, it promises to free man so he may develop his highest
capabilities, and to give him ethical standards so he may live
in harmony with himself, his neighbor and the world around
him. On the negative side, Madalyn insists atheism can thrive
only in a certain "social system." The political ramifications
are obvious: In order for man to reach his greatest potential,
the whole of society must be made to reject God.

The following quotations are other definitions of atheism
given by atheists and believers alike.

"Atheists deny that there is a Being called God who created the world, watches over man, knows their actions, hears
their prayers, cares for their needs, speaks in a whirlwind,
took upon himself flesh and walked upon earth and was seen
and heard and felt" (Charles Burton Martin, *Religious Belief*
[Ithaca: Cornell University Press, 1959], p. 4).

"Atheism, the deliberate, definite, dogmatic denial of the
existence of God . . . [it] is not satisfied with approximate or
relative truth, but claims to see the ins and outs of the game
quite clearly—being the absolute denial of the Absolute" (Etienne
Borne, *Atheism* [New York: Hawthorn Books, 1961], p. 8).

". . . the positive position of atheism, or non-theism . . . offers in the place of theism a rational way of life . . . and the opportunity for greater fulfillment of human potential. It promotes greater understanding and tolerance in social relations, logically, nationally and internationally" (William John Fielding, *The Shackles of the Supernatural* [Girard, Kan.: Haldeman-Julius Publications, 1938], p. 221).

"If God is defined to mean an existence other than the existence of which I am made, then I deny God. . . I deny the existence of such a being.

"Atheism is no mere disbelief; is no way a cold, barren negative; it is, on the contrary, a hearty, faithful affirmation of all truth, and involves the positive assertion of action of highest humanity . . ." (Charles Bradlaugh in Gordon Stein, ed., *An Anthology of Atheism and Rationalism* [Buffalo: Prometheus Books, 1980], p. 10).

". . . the universe . . . is all there is" (Peter Angeles, ed., *Critiques of God* [Buffalo: Prometheus Books, 1976], p. xiii).

"Atheism . . . is a denial of the major claims of all the varieties of theism. . . . Atheism is not to be identified with sheer unbelief" (p. 4). "[It] is a comprehensive account of the world believed to be wholly intelligible without the adoption of a theistic hypothesis" (p. 5). "Atheism is not simply a negative standpoint" (p. 15). (E. Nagel in Peter Angeles, ed., *Critiques of God*.) Nagel goes on to name materialism (p. 15), empiricism (p. 16) and utilitarian ethics (p. 16) as part of the atheistic belief system.

"Theists believe in God, while atheists do not have such a belief. [Atheists] believe in the existence of a physical universe composed of orderly atomic structures . . . [also] moral beliefs" (p. 11). "Atheism . . . is an intellectually respectable viewpoint" (p. 10). ". . . the atheist may claim to know that God does not exist" (p. 23). (B.C. Johnson, *The Atheist Debater's Handbook* [Buffalo: Prometheus Books, 1981].)

The above definitions represent the traditional understanding of atheism that has prevailed throughout the history of philosophy. Atheism, as we have seen, comprises an entire belief system, rather than just a simple, negative assertion. To be an atheist requires a commitment to certain philosophical positions such as materialism, situation ethics, empiricism, etc. They are the key ingredients of an atheist's belief system.

Atheists, as any other human beings, cannot help attempting to understand themselves and the world around them. The atheists' task, however, is to explain life without having to use the idea of God. They must try to develop ethical principles that will work without recourse to God or His revealed law. Such principles require a restructuring of society. The great atheistic philosophers, such as Marx, have always stated that a rejection of God cannot take place without a prior commitment to certain philosophical beliefs. These beliefs will logically lead the atheist to definite political ideas concerning how society is to be governed. And, we might add, over half of the world is now suffering under those political implications of atheism.

A Nonbelief

At this point, it would seem, we have gained enough information to define atheism. But we cannot omit a reference to one of the more eccentric definitions of atheism that pops up now and then when a public debate is staged between a theist and an atheist. Some atheists have learned by experience that it is quite impossible to prove a universal negative. If they denied outright that God existed, they would have to give some kind of proof for such an assertion. However, because this is logically and physically impossible, they have devised a way to escape having to prove anything: They redefine atheism.

According to one new definition, atheism is *not* the belief that God does not exist, for the atheist does not know that God does not exist. The atheist does not claim to know anything. He does not assert anything. He does not have any opinion on the matter whatsoever. Atheism is simply *the absence of belief in God*. Atheism has no beliefs or belief system. It does not attempt to understand or explain anything about anything. Thus, since atheism asserts nothing and has no beliefs or world view, it needs to prove nothing.

In *An Anthology of Atheism and Rationalism* (Buffalo: Prometheus Books, 1980), editor Gordon Stein opens the discussion with this novel approach:

> . . . an atheist is a person *without* a belief in God. The distinction is small but important. . . . To be without a belief in God merely means that the term "God" has no importance or possibly no meaning to you. Belief in God is not a factor in your life. Surely this is quite different from denying the existence of God. Atheism is not a belief as such. It is a lack of belief. (p. 3)
>
> If the atheist is simply without God, then he is not asserting anything. On the other hand, the theist is asserting the existence of something (God), so the burden of proof is on him. . . . Atheism is without God. It does not assert no God. The atheist does not say that there is no God. (p. 4)

One obvious contradiction to Stein's definition of atheism is the very title of the book in which he is writing. If atheism asserts nothing and believes nothing, why does he place "Rationalism" in the title? Evidently Stein would assert that rationalism is a valid belief system. The same can be said for the rest of the book. The contributors assert many beliefs such as materialism and ethical relativism, which they never bother to prove.

Atheists attempt this definition for only one reason: to allow themselves to bring in any ideas they wish without having to prove anything. But, in so doing, they have rendered atheism incapable of falsification or verification. And, if it is true (as they claim when attacking theism) that a word or an idea is nonsense if it is not capable of falsification or verification, then atheism is nonsense and should be dismissed as meaningless.

George Smith, in *Atheism: The Case Against God* (Buffalo: Prometheus Books, 1979), spends a great deal of time trying to establish that atheism need not be established:

> Atheism, therefore, is the absence of theistic belief . . . in its main form, it is not a belief; it is the absence of belief. (p. 7)
>
> If one presents a positive belief (i.e. an assertion which one claims to be true), one has the obligation to present evidence in its favor. The burden of proof lies with the person

who asserts the truth of a proposition. If the evidence is not forthcoming, if there are not sufficient grounds for accepting the proposition, it should not be believed. (p. 15)

The atheist *qua* atheist, whether implicit or explicit, does not assert the existence of anything; he makes no positive statement. Atheism is not the absence of belief in god plus certain positive beliefs: atheism *is* the absence of belief in god. (p. 18)

To view atheism as a way of life, whether beneficial or harmful, is false and misleading. (p. 21)

Smith's definition of atheism poses some problems, the first being the title of his book. When I publicly debated him I asked him why he entitled it *The Case Against God*? If it were true that atheism does not make any assertions about anything, how could he have a case against God? Where did the case come from? Doesn't making a case require many assertions?

He admitted he did not actually have any case against God *per se*. Since atheism is the absence of faith, he could not assert any cases whatsoever. What he meant was that theism did not have any proofs. He had to agree with me that the title of his book was a misnomer.

My second problem with Smith's definition is that if a simple absence of belief constitutes atheism, then virtually everything from rocks and tree stumps to dogs and cats would have to be numbered among the atheists. When a definition is so broad as to include almost everything, it usually means nothing. His definition is useless as well as meaningless.

My third problem with Smith's definition is how he can attempt to disprove the theistic proofs if he cannot make any assertion about anything. By what standards does he judge these proofs as invalid? On what basis and by what methods can he criticize the theistic proofs if he does not have his own belief system? Why does he have to appeal to such things as "logic" on page 61, and to "reason" on page 110? By doing this he is implying as his confession of faith, "I believe in logic. I believe in reason." He evidently asserts his belief in such things. When he says that every "advocate of reason must begin with an unequivocal condemnation of Christianity's brutal past" (p. 114), to make such moral judgments requires a prior commitment to ethical standards by which he can judge something. If he does not assert anything, however, he then cannot condemn anything.

This leads us to the fatal flaw in Smith's definition of atheism. Although he claims on page 21 that atheism does not have any additional beliefs or world view, he later reveals that he *believes* in the ethical teaching of Ayn Rand, the prophetess of selfishness (pp. 280–287). As part of his belief system, Smith believes "man is free to choose his actions, because he is not biologically programmed to act in a given manner" (p. 293). And on the basis of his belief in the humanistic ethics of Ayn Rand, he devotes the next chapter in his book to "The Sins of Christianity."

Again, after Smith claims on page 21 that atheism "does not imply any specific philosophical system" and that it does not give a "way of life," he contradicts himself on page 98 by stating:

> . . . in epistemological terms . . . atheism is the consequence of a commitment to rationality—the conviction that man's mind is fully competent to know the facts of reality, and that no aspect of the universe is closed to rational scrutiny. Atheism is merely a corollary, a specific application, of one's commitment to reason.
>
> I do not accept the existence of God, or any doctrine, on faith because I reject faith as a valid cognitive procedure. The particular content or object of faith—whether it be gods, unicorns or gremlins—is irrelevant in this context. The statement "I will not accept the existence of God on faith" is derived from the wider statement, "I will not accept *anything* on faith."
>
> Thus explicit atheism is primarily an epistemological position: if reason is one's only guide to knowledge, faith is necessarily excluded . . . theism is necessarily excluded.

Although he denied on page 21 that atheism is the result of a prior commitment to a world view, he reveals on page 98 that his atheism is in fact the result of a prior commitment to the nineteenth-century belief system called rationalism! His denial of God is merely a part of his belief in rationalism. While we are committed to rationality, we are not rationalists.

This last observation reveals why Smith and other such

atheists define atheism as an "absence of faith." By doing this, they can use their additional beliefs to condemn theism, yet escape having to prove these beliefs. It is like being robbed by a mugger with a gun in his hand as he tells you that he is unarmed.

It never seems to dawn on them that if atheism does not assert anything and has no beliefs, then no atheist could write a book in which he asserts that the theistic proofs are false. If atheists assert nothing, then they could write nothing.

Their attempt to promote beliefs such as rationalism, materialism, humanism, ethical relativism, etc., without having to prove the validity of these beliefs, opens them up to the charge of circular reasoning. For example, if someone assumes that materialism is true, any discussion they give to the question of God's existence is circular.

Premise: Since God does not exist,

Conclusion: therefore all that exists is matter.

Premise: Since all that exists is matter,

Conclusion: therefore God does not exist.

Since they begin with materialism, which is based upon the premise that God does not exist, they have already placed in their premise what they are going to place in their conclusion. Thus all of their arguments are circular in nature.

The only way they can honestly discuss the theistic proofs is by first revealing and proving the validity of their own belief systems such as materialism and rationalism. Instead of pretending to be "neutral" and "objective" and "free" from any beliefs, they should come clean and let people know what they believe.

They find this extremely difficult, however, because the systems they believe in arose with the beginning assumption that God does not exist. Since we have already seen this with materialism, ethical relativism can serve as another example of this problem.

Premise: Since God does not exist,

Conclusion: therefore moral absolutes do not exist.

Premise: Since moral absolutes do not exist,

Conclusion: therefore God does not exist.

Historically speaking, rationalism, materialism, etc., were belief systems developed by such thinkers as Hegel, Feuerbach, Nietzsche and Marx who *began* with the assumption that God did not exist. If there is no God, then all that exists is matter and man has only his own reason to guide him. But if there is a God, then materialism and rationalism are false beliefs. The attempt to define atheism as the absence of faith is thus seen as a feeble attempt to escape intellectual accountability for the belief systems which ultimately are based on atheism.

This is the secret of the triumphalism of modern atheists. They know that as long as they keep the discussion only on the level of the theistic proofs and never have to reveal or defend their faith in materialism, rationalism, etc., the contest between theism and atheism has been rigged from the beginning. There is no way for theism to win, for if a person begins with the assumption that God does not exist, he can only end with the conclusion that God does not exist. Circular arguments have always been as triumphal as they are fallacious.

A Definition of Atheism

Modern atheism or anti-theism is the product of various eighteenth and nineteenth-century philosophies or belief systems that defined reality in such a way that there was no place left for God in the universe. These same systems viewed belief in God as something detrimental to the welfare of mankind— if society and man himself is to be remolded into a paradise on earth, then belief in God must be removed from the minds of man, even by force.

Thus, modern atheism is not simply the absence of belief in God. It is actually an attack on God, a rebellion against God, and a challenge to God. This is the promethean fire which fuels the atheists' crusade against faith in God.

5

The Causes of Atheism

Having examined atheism as a belief, it is only natural to wonder why someone would choose to become one. After all, no one is born an atheist. One must *choose* to become one. And unless the atheist is willing to believe that his choice was totally due to irrational factors, he will have to admit that his choice to believe in atheism was shaped by various influences in his life.

Fear of Investigation

This line of thought is very disturbing to modern atheists. On the one hand, they want total freedom to examine the causes of theism, and are quite adept at attributing faith in God to a number of psychological problems. Freud was the first to use this approach. On the other hand, when this same method is applied to the atheists and the question is asked as to the causes of *their* unbelief, they suddenly reverse themselves and proclaim there is no need to examine the factors which cause someone to believe in atheism.

George Smith calls it "a dubious line of thought" which "deserves little comment."[1] He scorns such a procedure as "a feeble, almost laughable attempt."[2] He states, "The psychol-

---

[1]George H. Smith, *Atheism: The Case Against God* (Buffalo: Prometheus Books, 1979), pp. 22, 23.
[2]Ibid., p. 25.

ogizing of atheism, therefore, is irrelevant" because it will "accomplish nothing."[3] Smith's will to believe in atheism is so strong that he cannot allow any investigation into the causes of it. Of course, when he attacks theism, he has no problem applying the method to those who believe in God.[4]

Modern atheists such as Smith fear any investigation into the origin of their unbelief because they initially had only personal reasons for rejecting God. The personal reasons invariably came first and their adoption of materialism came later as a defense for a choice that they had already made.

Madalyn O'Hair is a good example of this point. When her life story was at last revealed by her son, it became obvious that she decided that she did not want to believe in God anymore when God did not give her what she wanted out of life. She had not gained the husband she wanted or the education she desired. Her family life was extremely miserable. So she turned against God with a savage fury. Later in life she picked up atheistic belief systems such as materialism and rationalism because these beliefs fit her original rejection of God.[5]

In the history of philosophy, the classic atheistic belief systems were developed by men who had already, for personal reasons, rejected God. Ludwig Feuerbach (1804–1872), for instance, was a theological student until he saw his two brothers cruelly treated by the police. His brothers, who had led a student revolt against the religion teachers in the university, were punished severely. Enraged with bitterness against his religious leaders, Feuerbach decided that he no longer wanted to believe in God if this was the way religious people treated his brothers. He vowed to get even by developing an attack on religion. His eventual philosophical system resulted from a prior personal rejection of God.[6]

The freethinker Jean Meslier (1664–1729) was forced into the priesthood by family pressure. Because of this, he devel-

---

[3]Ibid.
[4]Ibid., pp. 163f., 297f., etc.
[5]William Murray, *My Life Without God* (Nashville: Thomas Nelson, 1982).
[6]Vincent Miceli, *The Gods of Atheism* (Harrison, N.Y.: Roman Catholic Books, 1971), pp. 21, 22.

oped "a violent hatred and passionate disavowal" of religion. He later developed the idea that religion was the tool used by the state to keep the workers in slavery.[7]

Karl Marx (1818–1883) was the son of a wealthy Jew who converted to Christianity for business reasons. As Karl grew up he was rejected by his Jewish relatives because his parents had converted to Christianity, and by his Christian neighbors because he was a Jew. He never got over the burden of trying to live in two worlds, neither of which would accept him. His bitterness and hatred of religion knew no bounds. He frequently stated, "Criticism of religion is the foundation of all criticism."[8]

Auguste Comte (1798–1857) grew up in a home filled with conflict and confusion. He had extreme difficulties in his relationship with his strict Catholic parents, so he struck back at them when he was fourteen by announcing that he no longer cared to believe in God. Many years later he developed the belief system called Positivism which was based on his earlier atheism.[9]

Charles Bradlaugh (1833–1891) became a bitter enemy of religion because, as a youth, he had a bad experience in Sunday School. His teacher expelled him from the class because Bradlaugh was too rebellious. He was later thrown out of his strict religious home when he refused to accept the authority of his parents. In order to gain revenge against his church and family, he renounced God because he knew this would cause them much pain and grief.[10]

A close study of the lives of atheists who developed sophisticated attacks on religion usually reveals they had already, for personal reasons, rejected God long before becoming "freethinkers." The same can be said of modern anti-theists.

The well-known entertainer, Paul Winchell, freely admits

[7]*The Encyclopedia of Philosophy*, vol. 5, p. 283.
[8]Ibid., pp. 171, 172.
[9]Ibid., vol. 2, p. 173.
[10]Gordon Stein, ed., *An Anthology of Atheism and Rationalism* (Buffalo, N.Y.: Prometheus Books, 1984), p. 7.

that his savage attack on religion is rooted in his hatred of an orthodox Jewish upbringing. He claims that the religious teaching he received as a child turned his life into "a nightmare." In order to escape it, he "turned to drugs, alcohol and sexual debauchery."[11] He goes on to blame his mother and her religion for all the pain, frustration and failure in his life. He did not find peace of mind until he rejected God.[12]

Given the many atheists, agnostics, freethinkers, and other assorted infidels I have known through the years, in every single instance where I have been able to develop a friendship, the person has always admitted that his initial reasons for rejecting God were of a personal nature.

Given this situation, we may logically conclude that the causes of unbelief are a proper subject for study. The historical situation, social context, political pressures, economic factors, family conditions, and psychological factors all have a bearing on why a person chooses to reject God. Various studies have demonstrated this point.[13]

The question that naturally arises is why do modern atheists resist any examination of the when, where and why of their original rejection of God? A friend who was once an atheist supplied the clue: George (not his real name) confessed that his rejection of God was originally motivated by a desire to indulge in what his Christian parents called "immorality." In order to hurt his parents and to be free to do whatever he wanted, he renounced God. Later in life he became acquainted with atheistic belief systems which supplied him with intellectual reasons for his rejection of God. These reasons merely confirmed his personal rejection of God.

---

[11]Paul Winchell, *God Two Thousand: Religion Without the Bible* (Sylmar, Cal.: April Enterprises, 1982), p. ii.

[12]Ibid., p. 10.

[13]For such studies, see: Rocco Caporale and Antonio Grumelli, eds., *The Culture of Unbelief* (Berkeley: University of California Press, 1971); Susan Budd, *Varieties of Unbelief* (New York: Holmes & Meier Pubs., 1977); Jean Lacroix, *The Meaning of Modern Atheism* (New York: Macmillan, 1965); Ignace Lepp, *Atheism in Our Time* (New York: Macmillan, 1964); Robert Charles Sproul, *The Psychology of Atheism* (Minneapolis: Bethany House Publishers, 1974).

When I first met George, however, he pretended his atheism was the result of his study of philosophy. His pride kept him from admitting his real reason for adopting atheism. He wanted to maintain an air of intellectualism, but if he admitted that a gross desire for sex and drugs lay behind his initial rejection of God, this would not seem very "intellectual." But he freely admitted all this after we had developed a good friendship.

John (not his real name) is another example. He had been wrongfully kicked out of a Christian college and treated quite poorly because he had chosen to adopt various minor doctrines of which the faculty did not approve. Because of their unchristian behavior and their refusal to allow any freedom to disagree, John announced that he was now an atheist.

John's ill treatment at the hands of religious men turned him against all religion in general. While it was illogical to blame all religion, and God himself, for the acts of a few religious bigots, by denying the existence of God, John could strike back at a system which had oppressed him. He was bitter about his experience for many years, and, apparently, has never returned to the Church.

The obvious reason why atheists do not want any questions asked about the personal causes of their atheism is that such questions strip them of their facade of intellectualism, reducing them to simple human beings who rejected God because they were disappointed with or angry at Him.

Of course, this is not to say that all atheists denied God for the same reasons. The reasons vary with each person. Yet, there is always some painful confrontation, usually morally based, when, in order to live with himself, the person had to reject God so he could be free to do what he wanted. He could not be hypocritical about his lifestyle: If God be God then follow His rules for living; but if there is no God, then make and follow your own rules. In his mind, God simply had to go.

Varieties of Atheists

After many years of experience in dealing with atheists, I have concluded that there are several basic kinds of atheists.

The kinds listed below represent atheists that I, or others, have personally known.

There is, first of all, the Village Atheist. He is a colorful literary figure found not only in Mark Twain's writings but also in real life. One such atheist, Arnold, comes immediately to mind: a man disagreeable and quite nasty on almost any subject, but if someone has the misfortune to speak of God to him, his anger is unsurpassed. Arnold *knows* there is no God. He is quite straightforward and dogmatic about the issue. He is not interested in any theistic arguments because he already knows that there is no God—so how can there be any theistic proofs? He is opposed to Christmas and any other religious holiday. They would all be outlawed if he had his way.

This man is a colorful town character whose lifestyle is as bizarre as his beliefs. His constant companion and dinnermate is a store mannequin with whom he holds long conversations. His mannerisms are such that he has gained the reputation of being the village idiot as well as the village atheist. Needless to say, he has so far been unsuccessful in winning converts to his beliefs—or lack of them.

The second kind is the Bashful Atheist. Bob, for example, used to say he positively knew there was no God, until he was "shot down" by a sharp theist who demonstrated from logic that it was impossible to prove such a universal negative. To say with assurance that there was, is and never shall be any deity of any kind in the entire universe would require the atheist to travel throughout time, be everywhere at the same moment in time, and know all things. To do all this, he would have to be omnipotent, omnipresent and omniscient. In short, he would have to become the very God that he wishes so much to deny.

Once Bob saw that it was ridiculous to claim absolute knowledge that God does not exist, he became quite bashful about his atheism. He no longer claims he could prove that God does not exist. He simply states that he must begin with the assumption that God does not exist and if the theists can not come up with any proofs for the existence of God, then his assumption is correct. With this approach, he does not have to defend his atheism. He need only state that he assumes it to be true. He is soon going around in circles chasing his tail in endless circular arguments.

Premise: Since there is no God,

Conclusion: all theistic proofs are invalid.

Premise: Since the theistic proofs are invalid,

Conclusion: there is no God.

At first Bob, the Bashful Atheist, spent his time in the negative task of trying to think of ways to get out of the theistic proofs. His present position is that all questions about the origin, meaning or order of the universe, the dignity and purpose of man, morality and ethics, etc., are invalid questions and cannot be asked. He insists there are no answers to such questions unless one embraces the concept of God. Since no God exists, however, such answerless questions are a waste of time. He no longer engages in any debates on the subject.

The third kind of atheist is the Covert Agnostic. He is quite dogmatic that no one *can* know anything whatsoever about God. Of course, he does not realize that by saying this, he has hopelessly entangled himself in a logical fallacy. To say that God is unknowable is to *know* a great deal about God. The statement refutes itself.

There are two types of agnostics: ordinary and ornery. The ordinary agnostic says, "I really don't know if God exists. If you can show me from my own experience that such a God exists, I will believe in Him. I am open to believing in God." The ornery agnostic says, "I don't know anything about God and neither do you—no one can know anything about God. I am not open to believing in 'god' because the word has no meaning to me."

Alfred, one such Covert Agnostic, simply dismissed any word as "meaningless" if he did not like the meaning of it. He considered his understanding of a word as the only correct one. It was inconceivable to him that someone could have a greater or different understanding. To him, "god" was a word which had no meaning because he had set up such a narrow definition of "meaning" that "god" was automatically excluded. Even when theists told him that they understood the meaning of the word "God," Alfred rejected their meaning because it did not suit him.

Since the word "agnostic" comes from two Greek words (*a* + *gnosis*) which mean "no knowledge," and which form the root word for our English word "ignorant," I have never ceased to wonder how agnostics can speak so dogmatically on a subject upon which they claim to know nothing. How can they present themselves as authorities on a subject of which they are admittedly ignorant?

The fourth kind of atheist is the Professional Skeptic, examples of which I have encountered several times. This person is the proverbial gadfly who cannot resist taking the skeptical position on every issue. As Socrates proved a long time ago, it is easy to be a skeptic. The art of casting doubt on everything so that nothing can be known for sure is easy once a person gets the hang of it. The secret is to avoid having to give any arguments to support the skeptic methodology.

As a Professional Skeptic, Sid has been practicing his art for many years. He has made a career of poking fun at various philosophies, theism included. But I have never heard him make a positive statement about anything. Neither have I heard him acknowledge that the skeptic methodology is self-refuting. If "no one can know anything for certain," then how can we know for certain that this proposition is true? Sid and his fellow-skeptics are quite sure that they know that no one can know anything for sure!

The fifth kind is the Neurotic Atheist, a person who sometimes gets physically sick when people start to talk about God. He has an irrational revulsion to religion. If a church building is ahead of him he will cross the street in order to avoid walking near it.

Mary was obviously neurotic in her opposition to religion. She had been raised in a Christian home but fell into immorality when quite young. She eventually had an abortion, and when her family found out, she left home. The guilt over her immorality and the murder of her unborn child haunted her day and night. Instead of dealing with her guilt, however, she suppressed it until she became mentally confused.

I first met Mary in Greenwich Village, living a sad and miserable life as one of New York City's "bag ladies." At first she did not want to talk to me about God. She said, "There is no God, so leave me alone." After getting her into a woman's treatment center where her alcoholism and guilt could be exposed and healed, she not only became mentally balanced but she also became a Christian. When the emotional cause of her atheism had been cured, she no longer needed to be an atheist.

The sixth variety of atheist is the Paranoid Atheist. In this person the rejection of God is based on an irrational fear that God is persecuting him and is trying to kill him or throw him into hell. Religious people were hounding him and making his life miserable.

I was once mugged in New York City by such an atheist. At first, he told me there was no God, but later, he told me he knew God was going to throw him into hell. He blamed the ills of his life on the God he said did not exist. Of course, he did not make any sense. But that is the way with paranoid atheists. They rarely make sense.

The seventh kind of atheist is the God-Complex Atheist. I remember sitting in a living room listening to Steve, who confidently told me he could not believe there was anyone higher than himself who could command or judge his actions. The idea that there was some Superior Being to whom he was accountable was ridiculous to him. He said, "If there were a god, I would have to be it or him. After all, I am superior to God."

The Self-gratifying Atheist is the eighth kind, and he is part of a large group. Freud's rejection of God is no surprise once we learn that he made his wife move out of his bedroom so his sister could sleep with him. Huxley's claim that society immediately accept the theory of evolution because it gave people a way to indulge in immorality without guilt provides a perfect example of this kind of atheist.

Some kind of moral crisis usually precedes this person's choice of atheism. Be it drugs, sex, abortion, murder, stealing, or whatever, he chooses to get rid of God in order to gratify some lust of the flesh or mind. For example, when dealing with many homosexuals in Greenwich Village, I discovered an exceptionally large number of them were atheists. In almost every case the cause of the person's atheism was the conflict between religion and his particular sexual needs. One of them had to go.

The Marxist Atheist is the ninth kind of atheist. He is an atheist by necessity because this belief is part of the party line. This is sometimes a political necessity, such as when the state is putting theists into concentration camps. In such a case many people will feign atheism to avoid persecution. Atheism may also be an educational and economic necessity. For example, theists are excluded from higher education and desirable jobs in Communist countries. Some people have chosen to be atheistic in order to get a university degree or a better job.

As long as the concept of God exists in the minds of men, the state cannot exercise ultimate authority. The national leaders are accountable to God and thus must live moral lives and lead the nation in just ways. This would not fit into the Marxist practice of tyrannical dictatorship, so God must go. The denial of human rights is essential to the Marxist's goal. Human rights are based on a theistic world view in which people are viewed as having intrinsic dignity and worth as God's image-bearers. Thus, all people are endowed by their Creator with certain absolute rights. In order to get rid of these human rights, one must first get rid of God.

The last kind of atheist is the Fideistic Atheist. Here resides all manner of existential atheists who accept by blind faith that there is no God. They do not prove there is no God. They just take a leap of faith and declare that God is dead. Be they secularist atheists such as Sartre, or "religious" atheists such as Altizer, they all have one thing in common: the nonexistence of God is an article of blind faith. They all wish and hope there is no God.

The ten kinds of atheists we've described above depict the underlying motives of most modern atheists. I do not intend to be unkind in these descriptions. I only want to be as factual as possible according to my experience and research. After all, atheists are human beings, not machines. The reason they decide to swim upstream against the current of humanity by maintaining that there is no God deserves a close examination. It is this human side of their atheism that this chapter has exposed.

6

Logic and the Atheists

The relationship between modern atheism and logic is a precarious one. Beginning with the assumption that there is no God, and, hence, no absolute exists to serve as the basis for any other absolutes, the blight of relativism infected all fields of knowledge. Subsequent history has demonstrated that the spread of relativism is irresistible once the premise of atheism is assumed.

Premise: Since there is no God,

Conclusion: there are no absolutes.

Premise: Since there are no absolutes,

Conclusion: everything is relative.

The first field of relativization was ethics. The Ten Commandments, the Golden Rule and all other moral absolutes were jettisoned. With great joy, atheistic philosophers proclaimed that there were no moral absolutes. Ethics became a matter of personal preference instead of an issue of "absolutes." Morality was reduced until it had no more significance than a personal preference for vanilla over chocolate.

Joseph Lewis wrote in 1926, "There is in reality no absolute standard by which we judge. . . . In the final analysis our guide in moral affairs should be that which gives to the individual the greatest possible happiness."[1]

The *Encyclopedia Americana* comments, "Since there is no God, man is the creator of his own values."[2] John Hick declares, "There is no God; therefore no absolute values and no absolute laws."[3]

The poverty of relativism is demonstrated by its inability to condemn evil on an objective basis—when the existence of God was denied, the existence of good and evil was also denied. Its adherents must therefore depend on other bases of morality.

When confronted with the question (given his commitment to relativism), "On what grounds would you condemn the acts of Hitler?", the great infidel logician Bertrand Russell committed an obvious logical fallacy. He said that Hitler was wrong because "most people agree with me."[4] This is the fallacy called *argumentum ad populum,* in which something is considered true just because many people agree to it.

When Russell was finally forced to tell how he distinguished between good and evil, he said, "by my own feelings."[5] This is the logical fallacy known as *argumentum ad hominem* (circumstantial) in which something is said to be true simply because of the circumstances of the person. Russell was saying, "Because of *my* personal feelings, Hitler was wrong." Of course, if Russell's reasons were valid, Hitler could have argued on this same basis that he was right in killing six million Jews. His feelings and happiness were in complete accord with his actions!

At first people naively assumed that relativism could be contained in the realm of ethics. But relativism like a cancer could only grow until it had infiltrated *all* fields of knowledge. One by one, every area of knowledge has been infected and consumed by relativism. Several examples will illustrate this point.

---

[1]Joseph Lewis, *The Bible Unmasked* (New York: Freethought Publishing Co., 1926), p. 15.

[2]*The Encyclopedia Americana,* vol. 1, p. 604.

[3]John H. Hick, *The Existence of God* (New York: Macmillan, 1964), p. 186.

[4]Ibid., p. 185.

[5]Ibid., p. 183.

Relativism and History

Modern views of history have become relativistic. The idea that it is possible to have objective knowledge of the past has now been replaced by an agnostic approach to history which assumes no objective knowledge is possible. History, no longer a matter of historical facts, has been reduced to the level of subjective interpretation by the process that modern atheism unleashed.

Premise: Since there is no God,

Conclusion: there are no absolutes.

Premise: Since there are no absolutes,

Conclusion: everything is relative.

Premise: Since everything is relative,

Conclusion: history is relative.

Relativists view history as a matter of personal interpretation. No one can really know what happened in the past. History is therefore only relative, subjective interpretations which arise out of a historian's personal preference. The Soviets write history one way and the Americans write it another way, but it makes no difference in the end, for no one really knows what happened in the past. No one appeals to historical facts anymore because there are no absolutes in history.[6]

In this sense, modern atheists state that Jesus of Nazareth was not historical, i.e., His existence and teaching are not to be viewed as *facts* of history, but rather as the products of subjective interpretations. To be consistent, this principle should also hold true for Socrates, Napolean, Isaac Newton and Abraham Lincoln. After all, they are no more historical than Jesus. Each historian presents his subjective conception

---

[6]For an in-depth discussion of modern relativist historiographies, see: Gordon Clark, *Historiography: Secular and Religious* (New Jersey: Craig Press, 1971). David Hackett Fisher, *Historians' Fallacies: Toward a Logic of Historical Thought* (N.Y.: Harper and Row, 1970).

and not objective history. Thus all history is reduced to personal preference and interpretation.

Relativism and Science

The process of relativism has begun to erode confidence in the reality of scientific absolutes. What were once viewed as objective scientific laws which man discovered by observation and experimentation have now been relativized. This was unavoidable once atheism was adopted as the beginning assumption.

Premise: Since there is no God,

Conclusion: there are no absolutes.

Premise: Since there are no absolutes,

Conclusion: everything is relative.

Premise: Since everything is relative,

Conclusion: science is relative.

In one debate with an atheist, I asked, "What is a scientific 'law' or 'law of nature' to you?" He replied that a "law" is a statement written on a piece of paper which represents the ability of the human mind to order reality according to its wishes. There are no objective or absolute laws *per se* in the universe, so the order that we see in the world is a projection of our minds. There are no scientific absolutes.[7]

It was, of course, inevitable that once the laws of God were jettisoned, the laws of nature would soon follow. Western science was originally built upon the assumption that an orderly God had made an orderly universe which ran according to laws He had placed in it at creation. These laws were absolute because they were the laws of an absolute God. On one

---

[7]"The [scientific] patterns do not exist in nature; they exist inside our heads. . . . A so-called law of nature is really a human generalization about nature, which we then consciously, or unconsciously, project into an essentially ambiguous universe." Lee Carter, *Lucifer's Handbook* (Van Nuys: Academic Associates, 1977), p. 86.

occasion, Einstein was asked how he knew the speed of light in a vacuum was the same everywhere in the universe. He replied, "God does not play dice with this world." His answer was the same as that which Isaac Newton would have given. All scientific absolutes depend on the existence of an absolute God who upholds them throughout the universe.

The rise of relativism in quantum mechanics and modern physics has called all absolutes into question. Not even mathematics has been spared. Now there are no absolutes in math. Lee Carter, who wrote a handbook for atheists to use when debating theists, asserts:

> There are, then, no such things as eternal and necessary truths of arithmetic and geometry. . . . There are many possible systems of arithmetic and geometry. . . . But such mathematical propositions are only statements about the system we have set up.[8]

Carter is saying that $2+2=4$ is true only because we arbitrarily set it up that way. We could make $2+2=55$ if we wanted. There are no absolutes in math because everything is relative.

Science is now being defined in terms of subjective preference and cultural bias. The cancer of relativism has destroyed the soul of science.[9] The full implications of the relativization of Western science, however, are just beginning to manifest themselves. We now face an acute shortage of math and science teachers in the public schools. Students graduate from high school unable to solve the simplest mathematical problems. Very few young people have any desire to enter science as a career. The Western world's edge on technology has almost disappeared. The ultimate economic consequences of this decline may prove catastrophic for the Western world.

Relativism and Logic

The last bastion of absolutes was logic. But this too has been consumed by the same irresistible progress of unbelief

[8]Ibid., pp. 112, 113.
[9]For an example, see: Guy Zukav, *The Dancing Wu Li Masters: An Overview of the New Physics* (New York: Bantam Books, 1979.)

that destroyed absolutes in all other fields.

> Premise: Since there is no God,

> Conclusion: there are no absolutes.

> Premise: Since there are no absolutes,

> Conclusion: everything is relative.

> Premise: Since everything is relative,

> Conclusion: logic is relative.

Modern atheists are somewhat schizophrenic at this point. On the one hand, when confronted by a theistic argument that is logically valid, Carter advises young atheists to say, "Actually, logic is whatever people find to be convincing; and just as our concepts of nature have changed over the years, so have our concepts of the laws of logic."[10] He then dismisses Aristotle's law of contradiction "as childish sophistry" and goes on to relativize all logic by claiming that logic is a matter of personal preference. What is logical to me may not be logical to him. It is all relative.

On the other hand, when trying to refute the theistic proofs, the same modern atheists will suddenly reverse themselves and appeal to the absolute laws of logic. For example, when refuting theism, Carter will point out the invalid use of tautologies and other laws of logic (which he has declared relative).[11] On one page, he considers Aristotle's logic as "childish sophistry," while on another he employs it as the absolute truth!

Modern atheists never seem to realize that if there are no absolutes, then they cannot say theism is *absolutely* wrong. If there are no absolutes in history, science or logic, then it is impossible to say that history, science or logic refute Christianity. If everything is relative then theism is historically, scientifically and logically true to those who want it to be true. Atheists cannot objectively say that theism is false, for they

---

[10]Carter, ibid., p. 112.
[11]Ibid., p. 136.

deny objectivity. The irrational character of unbelief manifests itself most clearly in this issue. For example, how can atheists insist the law of contradiction to be invalid when they must use it to deny its validity? To declare "the law of contradiction is false" proves that the law is true.

If everything is relative, then all the arguments ever developed against the theistic proofs are invalid because they try to show that the theistic proofs are objectively or logically false. For if, as they claim, there is no objective truth, then there is no objective nontruth!

If modern atheists were consistent, they would say, "If the theistic proofs are logically valid to you, they *are* logically valid. If they are not logically valid to me, then they are *not* logically valid. It makes no difference. Logic is purely a matter of personal preference." But modern atheists are not consistent because they would be out of business if they were. They would never get any royalties because they would never write books. They could never obtain any teaching positions because they would have nothing to teach their students.

The idea that truth is like a lump of formless clay which can be molded any way one desires does not provide any ammunition against theism. Where then do the atheists derive their arguments? They must temporarily function on the very theistic base they are trying to refute. They must argue as if there were absolute truth. They must appeal to absolute laws in science, history and logic. If they don't do this, they can't argue. But to do so shows that their atheism, materialism and relativism are fideistic (relying on faith alone) in nature because their beliefs cannot be "proved" unless they adopt theistic methodologies. When they appeal to absolutes to prove that there are no absolutes, they reveal that their position is fideistic.

Another problem faces unbelief at this point. By its assumption of relativism, it has placed itself beyond verification or falsification. Since there are no absolutes to appeal to, atheists cannot prove their position nor can others disprove it. Since verification and falsification are two of their chief arguments against theism, on the basis of what they themselves believe, atheism is erroneous.

When someone points out the logical errors in their system, they can reply, "Logic is relative. I simply don't accept your rules of logic. I made up my own rules today and I am logical according to my rules. There are no absolutes in logic." The same fate awaits any attempt to point out the numerous historical or scientific errors in atheistic writings. The errors are dismissed as unimportant because "Everything is relative" or "It is only your personal opinion." In this way, the atheist cannot be refuted.

Of course, even if someone says there are no absolutes, he cannot live without absolutes. For instance, he must pay the proper amount at the check-out counter. Imagine him trying to convince the retailer that "everything is relative" and thus he will give the clerk one dollar for an item marked 25 dollars, and demand 150 dollars in change! In the same vein, who is going to jump off a ten-story building because the law of gravity is only relative?

The statement "Everything is relative" is not only unlivable, it is self-refuting, because it is always given as an absolute. (One student countered his infidel professor who had just said that everything was relative by asking him if he were *absolutely* sure of that!) "Everything is relative" is like the statement "Everything I say is a lie"; if everything I say is a lie, then the statement itself is a lie. My declaration means I must actually be someone who tells the truth. But if I always tell the truth, then how can I say that everything I say is a lie? The proposition is nonsense because it refutes itself.

The theist, however, is not fideistic because his faith is open to verification or falsification. When he states that the Bible is historically true, he means that it can be either verified or disproven by archaeological evidence. When the infidel Sir William Ramsey decided to disprove the reliability of the Bible, he went to the Middle East to do archaeological research. If the Bible were true he would find the evidence for such cities as Lystra, Derbe, etc., which were unknown at that time. But, on the other hand, if such cities never existed, then the Bible was false. His discoveries verified the reliability of the

Bible so strongly that he later became a Christian.[12]

Of course, most modern atheists will not accept any refutation from objective facts, even if they are empirical evidence from archaeology. In one of my radio debates with an atheist, the atheist argued that Nazareth did not exist because it was not mentioned by Josephus or the Talmud. I pointed out that:

1. She was arguing from silence, which is a logical fallacy. She was being irrational in her argument.

2. Neither Josephus nor the Talmud attempt to mention every city, town and village in Israel. Why should they mention a small village such as Nazareth?

3. Nazareth was mentioned in the New Testament which was written in the first century according to the empirical and internal evidence.[13]

4. The Nazareth Stone, bearing a decree by Claudius, was discovered in 1878. It can be dated A.D. 41–54.[14]

The atheist's response was instructive. She did not care if she was illogical in arguing from silence. As to the archaeological evidence I offered, she responded that "anybody can dig up a stone and call it whatever they want." She simply swept aside the archaeological evidence!

While someone can *say* that the laws of logic are relative and need not be followed, he must nonetheless *use* those laws to say it. Logic is essential to human thought and communication. The law of contradiction has an ontological (based upon an analysis of the nature of being) basis in the nature of the God who "cannot lie," and in the nature of man who was made in God's image. Since modern atheism is fideistic in nature, it has therefore become the task of the theists to de-

---

[12]Sir William Mitchell Ramsey, *The Cities of St. Paul* (Grand Rapids: Baker Book House, 1960).

[13]For the empirical evidence, see: David Estrada and William White, Jr., *The First New Testament* (Nashville: Thomas Nelson, 1978). For the internal evidence, see: John A.T. Robinson, *Redating the New Testament* (Philadelphia: Westminster Press, 1976).

[14]Roland Kenneth Harrison, *Archaeology of the New Testament* (New York: Association Press, 1964).

fend logic, reason and science.[15]

Of course, there is an appearance of reason in modern atheistic writings. When the typical modern atheist is refuting the theistic arguments, he will appeal to logic, reason and science because the arguments he is using came from the eighteenth and nineteenth century philosophers who believed in such absolutes. But when forced to defend his relativism, the modern atheist reveals that he believes there are no absolutes in logic, reason or science!

Modern atheists are thus in a hopeless situation. The only way they can refute the theistic proofs is by using old Kantian arguments which are based on absolutes which atheists no longer accept. It is a classic Catch-22 situation.

---

[15]For a theist's defense of logic see: *The Philosophy of Gordon Clark: A Festschrift* (Phillipsburg, N.J.: Presbyterian and Reformed Pub. Co., 1968), pp. 64–79. The writings of Francis Schaeffer, Ronald Nash and Robert Sproul also contain a defense of rationality.

7

Logical Errors of Atheism

M odern atheism's commitment to relativism has resulted in a careless attitude toward errors of logic and fact. In this chapter we will present some of the hundreds of errors found in current atheist literature. "Logical errors" refers to the *form* of the argument or the way the argument is *structured* or *stated*. Principles of logic determine whether or not an argument is *valid*; its truth or lack of falsehood is not the immediate concern, however, for while an argument may be valid and yet false, whatever is true is always valid.[1] Interestingly, the validity of the atheist's arguments does not depend on whether he is an atheist, agnostic or theist. An atheist committed to logic could have written this section of the book.

Error #1

It is erroneous to assume that refuting the opponent's theory will automatically prove my theory true. This is called *ignoratio elenchi* in which the argument I advance has nothing logically to do with my position. It is logically invalid to think that if I can disprove someone else, my position is true by default.

Most modern atheists commit this basic error. In his *Atheist*

---

[1]The discussion in this chapter will use the standard textbook in logic: Copi Irving, *Introduction to Logic* (New York: Macmillan, 1961).

Debater's Handbook, B. C. Johnson argues, ". . . the atheist need only demonstrate that the theist has failed to justify his position."[2] George Smith makes the same error in his book: "If we can show theism to be unsupported, false or nonsensical, then we have simultaneously established the validity of atheism."[3] Besides being a logical fallacy, several other problems arise with this approach. If the task of the atheist is to prove his position by refuting theism, then he has engaged himself in an endless negative procedure: He must refute *all* the arguments put forth by *all* theists of *all* kinds throughout *all* of history. And if he should succeed, he must not rest, for new arguments may have arisen while he was occupied with his earlier research. In principle, atheism will never be established because the task of refutation will never be completed.

The alternative is to commit another logical fallacy. If the atheist selects only the particular theistic arguments he knows he can handle, how can he say he has refuted theism? This is logically invalid because the attributes of a part cannot be attributed to the whole. This is called the fallacy of composition.

Or, again, what if his research is faulty? What if he may have selected a few weak arguments put forth by some uneducated theist? What if he is ignorant of the best defenders that theism has? What if his position is based on *argumentum ad ignorantiam*, i.e., ignorance of the position he is claiming to refute? This is the case with atheists such as Anthony Flew who does not seem aware of modern apologists; Flew's writings contain no references to E. J. Carnell, Gordon Clark, Francis Schaeffer, Van Til, John Warwick Montgomery, Ronald Nash, and other spokesmen for the faith.

Most atheists are ignorant of modern theism because they are still attacking the theistic proofs as formulated in the eighteenth century, and thus are using arguments devised by eighteenth-century atheists. Modern theists, however, have sharp-

---

[2]B.C. Johnson, *Atheist Debater's Handbook* (Buffalo: Prometheus Books, 1981), p. 12.
[3]George H. Smith, *Atheism: The Case Against God* (Buffalo: Prometheus Books, 1979), p. 18.

ened up their arguments to confront issues raised by atheists in the past. But the modern atheist, instead of dealing with contemporary restatements of the theistic proofs, will invariably dwell in the past.[4]

In addition to these problems, the atheist often does not understand what the theist is saying and thus misrepresents his argument. In such a case the atheist is only knocking down a "straw man" argument of his own invention. This is a major problem in statements by atheists such as Johnson, Smith and Carter. Most theists would not recognize what these men present as the beliefs of theism. This is another example of *ignoratio elenchi* (irrelevant conclusion).

The logical fallacies inherent in trying to prove one's position by refuting someone else's are too great to be overcome. It is an irrational procedure.

Error #2

It is erroneous to assume that merely giving an alternate explanation for something automatically refutes any other interpretation. Atheists often commit this basic error by assuming they have refuted miracles and religious experience by giving another explanation for them.[5] Explanation, however, is not to be confused with refutation. This is once again the fallacy of *ignoratio elenchi*.

As Copleston argued in his debate with Russell, to say, "I can explain that away" does not logically refute anything. One must *prove* his explanation; not simply state it.[6] Yet, this is a common procedure for atheists.

Error #3

It is erroneous to assume that the arguments for and against the existence of God have any logical or material bearing on

---

[4]For a restatement of the various theistic proofs, see: Alvin Plantinga, *God, Freedom, and Evil* (Grand Rapids: Wm. B. Eerdmans, 1974); Robert Sproul, John Gestner, Arthur Lindsley, *Classical Apologetics* (Grand Rapids: Zondervan, 1984).

[5]For examples, see: Johnson, ibid., p. 77; Smith, ibid., p. 18.

[6]John Hick, *The Existence of God* (New York: Macmillan, 1964), p. 189.

whether God exists or not. To assume that God does not exist because some of the arguments set forth by some theists may be defective or inconclusive is illogical. The existence of God, or anything else for that matter, does not depend on man's approval or disapproval. Once again this is *ignoratio elenchi.*

The philosophical error which underlies this erroneous assumption is the idea that reality must conform to what I think it to be. Whatever is unthinkable to me cannot exist. This was the erroneous foundation of the Rationalists of the eighteenth century. They believed they could sit in a darkened room and decide what did or did not exist out in the real world solely on the basis of what was "thinkable" or "unthinkable" to them. There was no need for experimentation or exploration. The mind alone could picture reality as it really was. There was no need to leave one's chair.

When the atheist concludes his refutation of some of the theistic proofs with the statement, "Now I know that God does not exist because I have refuted the theistic proofs," he is making an invalid conclusion. He can conclude that certain arguments are invalid, but he cannot logically conclude that God does not exist. The one has no logical bearing on the other.[7]

Error #4

It is erroneous to use arguments from silence to establish a position, for making positive pronouncements on the basis of silence is logically invalid.

We have seen in previous chapters that atheists frequently use this method in their attacks on the reliability of the Bible. For example, they erroneously concluded that there was no writing in Moses' day because it had not yet been discovered! They should have learned to stop making such logical blunders when archeologists discredited this argument against the Mosaic authorship of the Pentateuch. Sorry to say, today's

---

[7]For an example of this frequent error in atheist literature, see: Johnson, ibid., p. 23.

atheist literature is filled with numerous examples of this basic error in logic.

Error #5

It is erroneous to assume in a premise what is proven in the conclusion. Circular arguments are not valid proof for any position. This is called the fallacy of *petitio principii* (begging of the question).

The following examples of circular arguments, in addition to ones previously noted, are far too frequent in most atheist literature.

Example A

Premise: Since God does not exist,

Conclusion: there cannot be any evidence that He does exist.

Premise: Since there cannot be any evidence for God's existence,

Conclusion: all theistic evidences must be somehow false.

Premise: Since all theistic evidences are false,

Conclusion: God does not exist.

Example B

Premise: Since Jesus did not exist,

Conclusion: there can be no evidence that He did.

Premise: Since there cannot be any evidence for Jesus' existence,

Conclusion: all historical evidence for His existence must be fraudulent.

Premise: Since all historical evidence for Jesus is fraudulent,

Conclusion: Jesus did not exist.

Example C

Premise: Since there is no God,

Conclusion: no one can experience God.

Premise: Since no one has ever experienced God,

Conclusion: there is no God.

Example D

Premise: Since miracles do not exist,

Conclusion: no one has ever experienced a miracle.

Premise: Since no one has ever experienced a miracle,

Conclusion: miracles do not exist.

Example E

Premise: Since God does not exist,

Conclusion: "existence" is only of a material nature.

Premise: Since "existence" is only of a material nature,

Conclusion: God does not exist.

Example F

Premise: Since God does not exist,

Conclusion: all there is, is matter.

Premise: Since all there is, is matter,

Premise: and "meaning" is limited to what is,

Conclusion: then only material objects have "meaning."

Premise: Since "meaning" is limited to material objects,

Premise: and "God" is immaterial,

Conclusion: "God" has no "meaning."

Premise: Since "God" has no "meaning,"

Conclusion: then "God" does not exist.

The above circular arguments sometimes go undetected because the first premise is silently assumed. For example, Hume's famous argument against miracles is actually based on the circular reasoning found in Example D. Hume argues that since miracles are "contrary to firm and unalterable experience," they do not exist.[8] Yet, when Hume assumes that no one has ever experienced a miracle, he is already assuming what he has yet to prove. C. S. Lewis explains:

> Now of course we must agree with Hume that if there is absolutely "uniform experience" against miracles, if in other words they have never happened, why, then they never have. Unfortunately, we know the experience against them to be uniform only if we know that all the reports of them are false. And we can know all the reports of them are false only if we know already that miracles have never occurred. In fact, we are arguing in a circle.[9]

Error #6

It is erroneous to assume that the object of man's desires or wishes cannot exist. It is logically invalid to conclude that if a person has a strong emotional desire for something, the object of his desire must exist only in his mind, or that it will have no real existence apart from his wish.

This is the basic error of Feuerbach in his *Essence of Christianity* (1853). He argues that since God was something that man wished to believe in, something he felt he needed, therefore God was only the projection of man's wish or desire. God does not exist *per se*. Freud and many others have followed Feuerbach into this logical error.

---

[8]David Hume, *Enquiry Concerning Human Understanding* (La Salle, Ill.: Open Court, 1958), pp. 126–127.
[9]C.S. Lewis, *Miracles* (New York: Macmillan, 1947), p. 105.

Consider the application of this theory in a different context: Imagine that you have been awake all night in anxiety over the safety of a loved one traveling in the dark. With great emotion you desire and wish for the light of dawn. Can you validly conclude that the dawn will never come because it exists only as the wish of your desires? The dawn will come whether or not you wish for it. Your wishes and desires have no logical bearing on the existence of their object. In the same way, it is logically absurd to say that God does not exist because people feel their need of Him.

Feuerbach's argument can actually backfire. During a series of lectures I gave at James Monroe University in Virginia, one atheist student challenged me by declaring: "I can't accept Christianity because it is a psychological crutch. People believe in God only because He fills some emotional need they have." The student had combined Feuerbach and Freud into an argument against theism.

My response was as follows:

> I am glad that you admit in front of all these people that Christianity fills the psychological and emotional needs of man. Now if Christianity is true and it does really come from the God who made man in the first place, this is just what we would expect. After all, it stands to reason that the Creator would give a religion which would fit the needs of man.
>
> Now, as to the idea that God does not exist because He fills the needs of man, do you really believe that whatever fills the needs of man does not exist? If so, then you would have to deny the existence of a lot of things that you know exist.

The student stammered that he did not want to say Christianity filled the needs of man. I countered that if this is so, did he still hold to his previous objection? No, he did not hold to his original objection anymore. He had learned the bitter truth that he could not have his cake and eat it too.

Error #7

It is erroneous to assume that a word has meaning only if it fits one's personal definition of "meaning." To assume that all metaphysical words such as "God" do not possess any meaning, because materialism and empiricism are assumed true, is to argue in a circle as well as to misunderstand the nature of language. If a person dislikes the meaning of something, he simply denies it has any meaning. This is logically invalid.

This was a favorite argument with atheists for many years. Developed by A. J. Ayer in *Language, Truth and Logic,* it was used to "prove" that the words "God" and "God exists" are meaningless and pure nonsense. Even Russell used it in his debate with Frederick Copleston. Copleston's response is worth repeating:

> The proposition that metaphysical terms are meaningless seems to me to be a proposition based on an assumed philosophy. The dogmatic position behind it seems to be this: What will not go into my machine is nonexistent, or is meaningless.[10]

Copleston was right in pointing out that Russell was actually arguing in the circle described in Example E. While most modern atheists still use this argument, at least one modern atheist, George H. Smith, is honest enough to admit, "The principle on which Ayer based his rejection of theology is now considered defunct."[11]

Philosophers and logicians have pointed out that a host of logical fallacies lie behind Ayer's arguments.[12] Defining God out of existence is not the same as refuting the existence or meaning of God.

Error #8

It is erroneous to build one's position on self-refuting propositions. The following self-refuting propositions are from atheist literature or debates.

1. *Only empirically verifiable or falsifiable statements have any*

---

[10]Hick, ibid., pp. 170, 171.
[11]Smith, ibid., p. 30.
[12]For a recent treatment, see: Gordon Clark, *Language and Theology* (Phillipsburg, N.J.: Presbyterian and Reformed Pub. Co., 1980).

meaning. This statement is itself incapable of verification.

2. *There are no absolutes.* This statement is an absolute.

3. *Everything is relative.* This statement is meant to be taken as an absolute.

4. *We can't know anything with certainty.* Yet, we are supposed to know this statement with certainty.

5. *There is no truth.* Except, of course, the one just given.

6. *What a person believes is the result of irrational forces.* Then this statement itself is also the result of irrational forces. So, why believe it?

7. *What you believe is determined by psychological, environmental, chemical or class conditioning.* Then this belief also is the result of such conditioning as well, and is equally worthless.

8. *No one can know anything about God, for He is unknowable.* This statement requires a great deal of knowledge about God.

Error #9

It is erroneous to use "chance" as a "god of the gaps" methodology when faced with an argument one's position cannot explain. When confronted with issues they cannot explain, atheists usually resort to "chance" as the explanation, without demonstrating it to be a viable answer.[13] They consider it a valid answer to such questions as, "How did the universe begin?", "How did life begin?", "Why is man unique?" Generally, their flippant answer is, "Why, chance explains it all. It all happened by chance." They do not attempt to *prove* the validity of "chance." To the atheist "chance" explains all, does all, and is the basis of all things. This appeal to "chance" is logically fallacious for several reasons.

First, "chance" is a nonanswer. It is an example of the fallacy of "false cause" and "amphiboly" (ambiguity). The atheist is careful never to define what he means by "chance." He merely identifies it as the cause of all things. It is a nonanswer.

For example, the noted infidel Robert Ingersoll had de-

---

[13]Peter A. Angeles, *Critiques of God* (Buffalo: Prometheus Books, 1976), p. 350.

cided to visit a new model of the solar system at the New York Planetarium. A scale model of the sun with all the planets moving in orbit around it was suspended from the ceiling.

When Ingersoll entered the room and saw the display, he exclaimed, "This is beautiful! Who made it?"

The head of the planetarium, a theist, who was escorting Ingersoll, said, "Why, no one made it. It just suddenly appeared by chance in this room one day." Reportedly, Ingersoll laughed because he saw for the first time the absurdity of attributing the universe to "chance." Just as "chance" was a nonanswer to the origin of the model of the solar system, it is even more of a nonanswer when applied to the origin of the universe itself.

Second, "chance" is the wrong answer. If, by "chance," the atheist is referring to the laws of probability and statistical averages, there are certain mathematical limits to what "chance" can and cannot do. "Chance" simply cannot be the omnipotent and infinite thing that the atheist wishes it to be.

Various concepts support this view. According to Lecomte Du Nouy, in *Human Destiny*, every statistical study into the probability of the universe (with all its complexity), and life itself, coming into existence by chance alone has demonstrated zero probability of that happening. It is also an unalterable scientific law that what chance creates, chance destroys. Chance is never the cause of order. It always produces disorder.

Third, "chance" is also a bad answer. It means man is a meaningless accident. No wonder Russell called man "a curious accident in a backwater,"[14] and another atheist concluded, ". . . the universe and human existence in it are without a purpose and therefore devoid of meaning."[15]

The Nazis and the Marxists have demonstrated the practical consequences of the view that human beings are without meaning, purpose or value. That view has resulted in more people being brutally murdered in this century than in all the

---

[14]Ibid., p. 296.
[15]Johnson, ibid., pp. 32, 55, 58; Carter, ibid., pp. 96–100.

wars of all of history combined. This is why we think "chance" is a bad answer.

Error #10

It is erroneous to assume that if a system contains beliefs which predate the system, the system is therefore false. One of the more popular arguments heard today on college campuses is that Christianity is false because some of its concepts, such as a substitutionary atonement, actually predate Christianity.[16] In one radio debate with an atheist, the atheist told me with glee that there were fourteen crucified saviors before Christ appeared on the scene. From this he concluded that Christianity was false. My response included the following points:

1. I have yet to see any empirical or literary evidence for this theory; no one has yet presented a shred of evidence from a pre-Christian source. Where is the proof that such concepts existed before Christ?[17]

2. If some of the concepts of Christianity existed before in the Jewish religion, or in the pagan religions which had contact with the Jews, so what? Would not God prepare people for the coming of the Christ and the work He was to do? Doesn't the New Testament claim to be built on the Old Testament? Where in the New Testament do the Apostles or Jesus claim they were totally original in all their ideas?

3. Was Copernicus' theory false because others predated him with the idea of a heliocentric universe? Must all systems be totally unique? Are they invalid if they build upon previous ideas? Such an argument is absurd.

Error #11

It is erroneous to assume that reality must conform to personal experience. Just because a person has not experienced

[16]Carter, ibid., pp. 79, 152, 153.

[17]For a recent update on this issue, see: Edwin Yamauchi, *Pre-Christian Gnosticism: A Survey of the Proposed Evidences* (Grand Rapids: Baker Books, 1983).

something does not mean he may logically assume no one else has experienced it or that it does not exist. This is the error of arbitrarily making a universal out of a particular, and is called a "hasty generalization."

Here are examples of the hasty generalization: "I tried praying to God once but did not get what I asked for. Therefore prayer does not work"; "I challenged God to strike me dead if He existed. Since He did not do it, He does not exist"; "Because of my bad experience with religion, I know all religion is harmful." The underlying error in these arguments is the assumption that one can take his own personal experience and make it a universal.

A more sophisticated form of this error is found in the argument that the only way we could ever know if God were good is for us to know Him by way of a personal relationship or friendship. But, since no one can know God personally, then no one can say God is really God.[18]

In addition to being trapped in the circular argument found in Example C, however, the user of this argument is actually saying that since *he* has never personally known God, therefore no one else has either. He is attempting to make his own personal experience universal. This is logically invalid.

The argument is also materially false because millions of people have claimed that they have a personal relationship with God. The impossibility of friendship with God would come as a great surprise to Abraham, who was called "God's friend" (James 2:23). The biblical call, "Taste and see that the Lord is good" (Ps. 34:8) is still being verified today.

Error #12

It is erroneous to use fallacies of ambiguity or equivocation in which the atheist introduces a different meaning to a word which is being used by the theist in his argument. Modern atheists often redefine the terms in a theist's argument in order to escape having to admit that the theist is right. For ex-

---

[18]Johnson, ibid., p. 99; Carter, ibid., p. 78.

ample, when the theist argues, "Without God, it is impossible to have morals, truth or meaning," he is defining the words "morals," "truth" and "meaning" in a specific way. He is referring to absolute, eternal, objective, essential and transcendent morals, truth and meaning. Man is not the creator or the measure of such things. They do not depend upon man's wishes, desires, ideas, background, situation or culture. What is immoral *is* immoral, whether anyone cares to accept the standard or not. The same holds for truth and meaning.

This is the underlying problem with most of Anthony Flew's arguments. He, as Nielson in his *Ethics Without God*, commits the fallacy of equivocation by redefining the terms which the theist has used. When he responds to the theist that he has morals, truth and meaning without God, he never informs his reader that he has switched the meaning of those terms. Thus his answer does not relate to the challenge of the theist. The words are the same but the meaning has changed. This is the logical fallacy of equivocation.

The equivocation is found in that the atheist's meaning of "morals," "truth" and "meaning" is the opposite of what the theist means by these terms. The following chart illustrates the differences.

EQUIVOCATION OF "MORALS," "TRUTH" AND "MEANING"

Theist	Atheist
absolute	relative
eternal	temporary
objective	subjective
essential	existential
transcendent	cultural

The relativism of atheism means the destruction of morals, truth and meaning in the sense the theists are using these terms. The fallacy of equivocation helps the atheist escape having to admit to the average person that without God it is not possible to have morals, truth or meaning. This reveals the lengths to which anti-theistic prejudice will go.

Error #13

It is erroneous to argue from the basis of such logical fallacies that appeal to pity (*misericordia*),[19] improper analogies,[20] *ad hominem* arguments (attacking the man),[21] and confusing "how" and "why" questions.[22]

Modern atheistic literature is filled with such fallacies. Indeed, *The Encyclopedia of Unbelief* (Buffalo: Prometheus Books, 1985) illustrates every logical, historical, scientific and biblical fallacy known. After surveying the literature, one gains the impression that modern atheists are so desperate to refute theism that they will use any and all arguments, regardless if they are logically invalid.

The willingness of modern atheists to violate the laws of logic is most clearly shown in their attempt to prove the theory of evolution. For example, one of the more recent popular arguments for evolution is that since humans and chimpanzees are similar in the structure of their chromosomes, therefore man evolved from the chimpanzee, or man and chimpanzee evolved from a common origin. Sometimes "ape" replaces "chimpanzee" but the form of the argument remains the same.[23] When the argument is reduced to its syllogistic form, the evolutionist is actually saying:

Premise: If X is similar to Y in Z,

Conclusion: then X evolved from Y

or

X and Y evolved from K.

---

[19]Johnson, ibid., pp. 85f.
[20]Carter, ibid., pp. 13, 27, 28, 55, 75, 78, 80, etc.
[21]Johnson, ibid., pp. 17–20.
[22]Johnson, ibid., p. 106.
[23]See: *Science* (April 11, 1975, vol. 188; June 6, 1980, vol. 208); *Nature* (Nov. 16, 1978, vol. 276).

The absurdity of this line of reasoning seems obvious, because the form of the argument is logically invalid for several reasons. First, the conclusion has no relationship to the premise; the law of the excluded middle applies in this situation. Second, the attributes of a part cannot be applied to the whole; that two organisms share similar features does not logically imply that as whole beings they had a similar origin. Third, the conclusion could have just as easily stated that Y (i.e. chimpanzees) evolved from X (i.e. humans); there is no reason that X should have evolved from Y. Fourth, the word "similar" is not the same as "identical"; the evolutionists fail to avoid the fallacy of equivocation.

Even if the form of the evolutionist's argument were granted, it would result in absurd positions. For example, humans and giraffes are similar in that they possess the same number of vertebrae in their necks. Can we conclude from this that man evolved from the giraffe or that man and the giraffe have a common origin? Of course not.

Lastly, the evolutionist is assuming that the presence of similar or identical designs or processes in life forms on this planet somehow is against Creation. Yet, the theist has always pointed to designs as proof of an intelligent Designer! The evolutionist is actually using the theists "argument from design." This he cannot do as a chance-produced universe should not manifest order and harmony but confusion and chaos.

We can go one step further. Some atheists deliberately use deception to refute theism. Why else, apparently, would Prometheus Books, the main atheist publisher, produce *The Art of Deception*, which instructs its reader to use any invalid or deceptive argument as long as it helps him to win his case? Consider some of the advice *Art of Deception* gives:

> Never admit defeat. . . . (p. 117)
> Refuse to be convinced. Even if you feel that he has a good argument and that your case is weaker, refuse to be convinced of your opponent's case. (p. 117)
> There is one thing you should always claim no matter what the opposition has said, namely, that the opposition has misstated your case. No matter what the opposition has said, you should make this claim. (p. 118)

Appeal to ignorance . . . act as if you are absolutely right. Keep harping upon the fact that some of the things you have said, even if they are trivial, are right and that the opposition cannot disprove your case. (p. 120)

Defense of Generalization. . . . the defense against the charge of a hasty generalization (or the existence of an exception to your generalization) is to fall back on the wise saying that "the exception proves the rule" and hope for the best. This, by the way, implies (but do not tell anyone about it) that the more exceptions there are the better is the rule. That does sound strange! Actually, the original statement was made by Francis Bacon and when he said it the word "prove" meant "test." You test a generalization by looking for exceptions. Rather than helping the generalization, the exception invalidates it. (p. 124)

Quoting Out of Context. Like any other charge, this one should be denied and continually denied. Keep insisting that the words you quoted are exactly as you said they were, that is, you ignore the charge that you quoted out of context and pretend that you were charged with misquoting. (p. 125)

Inconsistency. If you are accused of being inconsistent, deny it! Deny it! . . . there may be times when inconsistency is not a bad thing. . . . Didn't the famous German philosopher Hegel deny the law of the excluded middle which is the logical foundation of inconsistency? All right, then I am inconsistent. So what of it? (p. 127)

Red Herring. . . . What happens if you feel that your defense has not been strong enough or that there are lingering doubts in the audience? At this point you should avoid sticking to the point. . . . draw attention to a side issue where you feel particularly strong. This will give the impression that you are still in charge of the course of the conversation. (p. 128)

Ad Hominem. . . . Instead of attacking the specific points of an argument, you attack the man. (p. 137)

True by Definition. You can always save your position by making it true by definition. (p. 141)

The above advice provides a small sampling of the "dirty tricks" methodology that seems to pervade modern atheism. While the atheists of the nineteenth century tried to be logically valid, modern atheists will use anything in their arguments, including the deliberate use of logical fallacies. My personal experience has proven this makes rational debate with an atheist very difficult.

Summary

When reading or listening to arguments by modern atheists, it is important to begin by scrutinizing the internal structure of the argument to see if there are any hidden presuppositions of logical fallacies. This applies to both theists and atheists. Belief or unbelief has no bearing on the validity of an argument.

In the atheistic literature I have read, circular reasoning appears more often than any other logical fallacy. Arguing in a circle is much like rowing a boat with only one oar—you never get anywhere! Nonetheless, they keep rowing.

While theism is not automatically established because of errors found in the atheistic arguments examined here, we can logically conclude that, insofar as our research has been completed, the basic logical flaws discussed in this chapter do form the basis of the main arguments that modern atheists use in their crusade against God. And if the basis of an argument is logically invalid, the argument built on that basis is false.

8

Materialism

One assumption underlying modern atheism is the philosophical system called materialism. Essential to the atheist's world view, this belief forms his basic attitude toward man and his place in the universe.

The word "materialism" is used in various ways. Its most popular usage refers to people guilty of greed and avarice, a "materialist" being someone whose life revolves around his material possessions.

The other major definition of "materialism" is used in a philosophical and technical sense, referring to those who reduce or limit reality to material objects. Their creed is, "Everything that is, is material." By this they mean that anything not of a material nature does not exist, and is only a figment of man's imagination. Thus God, by definition, does not exist. Man himself is only a material machine with no soul or spiritual essence. Everything that is man is material. In this chapter we will use the word "materialism" in this second sense.

Materialism and Empiricism

As a philosophic world view, materialism assumes the validity of the theory of empiricism. Thus materialism is a view of being which depends on a certain view of knowing. Empiricism states that knowledge must be restricted to those objects which can be perceived by our senses. Thus we cannot "know" nonmaterial objects. Materialists go one step further and state that since we cannot know nonmaterial things, we must conclude that these things do not exist. It is therefore a waste of time, because meaning is restricted to what we can know, which is reduced to material objects which can be perceived by the five senses.

The relationship between materialism and empiricism, however, is not a logical one in which one is validly deduced from the other. The materialists' argument, "Since we cannot know anything about nonmaterial objects, therefore they do not exist," is invalid. One may validly deduce from the principle of empiricism *only* that nonmaterial things are unknowable. To say that nonmaterial things do not exist is to know too much. Rather, materialism and empiricism are related on a presuppositional level where both are faith assumptions. And they are also related historically in that the popularity of empiricism paved the way for the acceptance of materialism.

A Brief History[1]

The philosophic world view of materialism first appeared in the writings of Democritus (460–360 B.C.), who was called "the Father of Materialism."[2] He stated as his creed, "Everything that is, is made of atoms." As the first true materialist, he denied that the atoms were acted upon by forces such as "mind," "love," and "hate." While Empedocles and Anaxagoras believed in nonmaterial forces, Democritus believed that atoms moved because of their own innate powers. He thus denied the existence of any nonmaterial forces.

Materialism did not reappear until the seventeenth-century Renaissance when the Greek classics were rediscovered and began to influence such writers as Gassendi (1592–1655)

---

[1]For a detailed study of materialism, see the classic work, *The History of Materialism*, by Frederick Lange (London, 1925). Also see: Paul Edwards, ed. *The Encyclopedia of Philosophy* (New York: Macmillan, 1977). Wilhelm Windelband, *A History of Philosophy* (New York: Harper & Row, 1958).

[2]Edward Zeller, *Outlines of the History of Greek Philosophy* (New York: Meridian Books, 1967), pp. 80–86; D. Runes, *Dictionary of Philosophy* (New Jersey: Littlefield, Adams & Co., 1967), p. 75.

and Hobbs (1589–1679). Hobbs, the more consistent of the two, denied the existence of all nonmaterial things, including God, souls and angels.

In the eighteenth century, Julien de Le Mittrie (1709–1751) crystalized the concept of man as machine, while the anti-Christian materialist d'Holback (1723–1789), desiring to escape the theistic implication of creation *ex nihilo*, strove to establish the eternity of matter. For the first time, materialism was beginning to experience popularity.

During the nineteenth century, materialists such as Ludwig Buchner (1824–1899) taught that there is no force without matter and no matter without force. The evolutionist T. H. Huxley (1825–1895) did much to popularize a materialistic view of the origin of life that involved spontaneous generation, i.e., life out of nonlife.

When the twentieth century dawned, the philosophy of materialism began to exercise an iron grip on state universities and colleges. Writers such as Gilbert Ryle attempted to refute the idea that there is a "ghost," i.e., a soul or mind, in the machine called man.[3] Finally, in the 1970s–1980s, the grip of materialism began to weaken under the assault of modern brain research, parapsychological experiments and quantum mechanics.

As a philosophy, or world and life view, materialism must satisfy the same demands of reason and experience demanded of any other philosophy. No amount of special pleading can exempt materialism from a rigid philosophical analysis. Using the kind of questions (which I developed in an earlier book) which should be applied to all systems of thought, we will apply some of these questions to the philosophy of materialism.[4] This analysis will have three divisions. First, we will analyze the internal integrity of the theory of materialism, thus, we will examine the theory itself. Second, we will analyze the theory as it relates to the world around us. Third, we

---

[3]Gilbert Ryle, *The Concept of the Mind* (London: Oxford Press, 1949).
[4]Robert Morey, *A Christian Handbook for Defending the Faith* (Phillipsburg, N.J.: Presbyterian and Reformed Publishing Co., 1979).

will analyze the theory as it relates to its understanding of man.

The Internal Integrity of Materialism

Materialists have not solved all the inherent self-refuting elements and logical fallacies found in their system. When confronted by the lack of internal integrity in their system, most modern materialists reply that materialism is not really a system but only the best guess available. They have become "shy" about their materialism. This is in stark contrast to the bold dogmatics of the materialists who went before them. This modern insecurity has risen from their growing awareness of inherent problems in the theory. I will detail five of these problems.

1. Materialists fail to recognize that their system is based on metaphysical assumptions.

Every system has its "first principles," or foundational presuppositions upon which it is based, and materialism is no exception. Yet, because these presuppositions are not material in nature or demonstration, materialists become very nervous when confronted by them. The following is a list of faith assumptions or presuppositions of materialism:

a. Materialism assumes the doctrine of human autonomy. Human autonomy is the theory that man, starting from himself and by himself, can understand man and the world around him without any supernatural revelation or information. "Man is the measure of all things," and man can build a unified system of knowledge by which everything can be explained. The tragic history of philosophy, in which each system refutes the ones going before it, should have taught materialists the invalidity of the theory of human autonomy. Human autonomy always ends in skepticism, i.e., reason cannot come to any conclusions at all.

b. Materialism assumes the theory of empiricism is true. Its adherents fail to see that empiricism is self-refuting. The theory that all knowledge is limited to what can be empirically known is itself incapable of being known or demonstrated on empirical grounds.

c. Materialists assume we are living in a closed universe in which everything, in principle, is explainable in material categories. When confronted by evidence for nonmaterial realities, they end up arguing in a circle by asserting such things do not exist because they do not exist. The concept of a closed universe leads to a closed system and a closed mind which argues, "Don't confuse me with the facts; my mind is already made up."

d. Materialists assume the doctrine of ontological thinking, i.e., reality must conform to what they think it to be. Anything which is unthinkable to them cannot exist. They thus reduce or limit reality to what their finite minds can grasp. Since they philosophically reduce reality to material objects, they assume that nonmaterial objects—"unthinkable" in material terms—cannot exist.

Uncovering the metaphysical assumptions of materialism reveals its religious commitment to a mechanistic, closed universe. The presuppositions are groundless because they are not rooted in human experience. They are leaps of faith. While they reject metaphysics, materialists cannot escape building their system upon it.

2. *As theory, materialism is self-refuting.*[5]

C. S. Lewis, in *Miracles*, reveals the self-refuting character of the main premise of materialism:

> . . . no account of the universe can be true unless that account leaves it possible for our thinking to be a real insight. A theory which explained everything else in the whole universe but which made it impossible to believe that our thinking was valid would be utterly out of court. For that theory would itself have been reached by thinking, and if thinking is not valid, that theory would, of course, be itself demolished. It would have proved that no argument was sound—

---

[5]For an investigation of the self-refuting nature of materialism, see: Paul Badham, *Christian Beliefs About Life After Death* (New York: Barnes & Noble, 1976), p. 4; *King's College Lectures on Immortality* (London: University of London Press, 1920), p. 130.

a proof that there are no such things as proofs—which is nonsense.

. . . no thought is valid if it can be fully explained as the results of irrational causes.[6]

But Naturalism, as commonly held, is precisely a theory of this sort. The mind, like every other particular thing or event, is supposed to be simply the product of the Total System. It is supposed to be that and nothing more, to have no power whatever of going on to its own accord. And the Total System is not supposed to be rational. All thoughts whatever are therefore the results of irrational causes, and nothing more than that.

. . . The Naturalist will have to admit that thoughts produced by lunacy or alcohol or by the mere wish to disbelieve in Naturalism are just as valid as his own thoughts. What is sauce for the goose is sauce for the gander. The Naturalist cannot condemn other people's thoughts because they have irrational causes and continue to believe his own which have (if Naturalism is true) equally irrational causes.

Thus the Freudian proves that all thoughts are merely due to complexes—except the thoughts which constitute this proof itself. The Marxist proves that all thoughts result from class conditioning—except the thought he is thinking while he says this.[7]

If all thoughts have irrational causes, then that thought itself has an irrational cause. So why should we believe it? If all thoughts are irrational chemical secretions or electrical charges, then why should the thought of materialism be viewed as rational and reasonable?[8] As Lewis eloquently points out, the materialists want to refute Christian thoughts by tracing them supposedly to irrational causes such as chemical determinism, behavioral conditioning or class consciousness. But they exempt themselves. This they cannot logically or rationally do.

3. *Materialism is not coherent.*

The theory states that reality is made solely of matter or objects which have material properties. The whole theory turns

---

[6]C.S. Lewis, *Miracles* (New York: Macmillan, 1966), pp. 20–21.

[7]Ibid., pp. 21–23.

[8]Paul Edwards and Arthur Pap, eds., *A Modern Introduction to Philosophy* (New York: Free Press, 1965), p. 177.

on the word "matter" or "material." Yet, this is exactly where materialism's incoherence reveals itself. No one seems to know what "matter" or "material properties," means. They cannot define matter.[9]

Modern physicists long ago abandoned the artificial Newtonian models of atoms and molecules. Modern physics has led us to a crisis in which no one seems to know what matter is. As a theory, materialism was coherent in the nineteenth-century context of a belief in "celestial ether," but it is incoherent in the context of modern physics.

4. Materialism uses circular reasoning.[10]

When confronted by evidence of nonmaterial realities, a materialist probably will "refute" such evidence by merely redefining it in materialistic terminology. Just because he redefines something, however, does not mean he has refuted it. Yet, this is the common practice of materialists. For example, when a materialist was confronted by the sober testimony of a credible witness who had experienced an angelic visitation, the materialist failed to recognize that *giving* an alternate explanation is not the same as *proving* that alternate explanation.

5. Materialism cannot validly speak of the world or the universe as a totality.

If human knowledge is limited to what the senses can perceive, who has ever been able to see all of reality in one-sense perception? Who can step outside of the cosmos to look at it objectively? And would not the person who "steps out" be part of this reality? How can the materialists talk about "ultimate reality" without contradicting their own position? Have they ever seen it?

Materialism holds, inherent within itself, the seeds of its own destruction. James Balfour stated it beautifully in 1895 when he said:

What sort of a system is that which makes haste to dis-

---

[9]Edwards, ed., *Encyclopedia of Philosophy*, Vol. IV, p. 179.
[10]Edwards and Pap, *A Modern Introduction to Philosophy*, p. 177.

credit its own premises? In what entanglements of contradictions do we not find ourselves involved by the attempt to rest science upon observations which science itself asserts to be erroneous?[11]

Materialism and the World

Materialism attempts to give a plausible explanation of the origin and nature of the universe. Popular TV series such as Carl Sagan's *Cosmos*, Kenneth Clark's *Civilization*, and David Attenborough's *Life on Earth* each exemplify a dogmatically materialistic world view. Virtually every college and high school textbook presents the theory of materialism as a fact and ignores any other viewpoint. The writers assume their world view is the only plausible one and that it alone should be presented in secular education. As a system, it seems to generate arrogant, pretentious attitudes among its adherents, preventing them from being open to contrary evidence.

While the materialists assume that they have developed a completely satisfying explanation of the universe, five major defects in their world view render it highly questionable.

1. Materialism is simplistic.[12]

To sweep away all the complexities of this world and put forth the maxim, "Whatever is, is matter," demonstrates the grossest simplicity. The universe is far too complex and varied to be the dull world of matter which the materialists claim it to be.

2. Materialism is guilty of reductionism.[13]

The method or process of reductionism selects one element of reality as absolute and reduces the rest of reality to that one category. Anything not reducible is relegated to nonexistence. This process reduces man to the status of a stone, for every-

[11]Arthur Balfour, *The Foundations of Belief* (New York: Longmans, Green and Co., 1895), p. 113.

[12]Bernard Ramm, *The Christian View of Science and Scripture* (London: Paternoster Books, 1964), p. 39.

[13]Ibid., p. 40.

thing has the same material, there being no qualitative distinctions between objects.

While idealists such as Berkeley reduce reality to "mind" and deny the existence of "matter," the materialists reduce reality to "matter" and deny the existence of "mind"! Both, of course, assume reality must be of only one being, thus conforming to the metaphysical theory of monism. They are both guilty of reductionism. But on what grounds do they assume reality must be of only one kind of being? Why cannot reality be of both matter and mind? Why do they demand that we must choose one over the other?

3. *Materialism is inadequate to explain the origin of the universe.*[14]

First, if (as the materialists claim) all knowledge is restricted to what our senses can perceive, then no one can logically discuss the origin of the universe or life because no person alive was there to perceive it. When they talk about origins, materialists have entered the realm of religion and metaphysics. Second, the materialists have yet to adequately explain why anyone should accept the astounding premises they present to account for the origin of the universe and life. They would have us accept:

a. Everything ultimately came from nothing.

b. Order came from chaos.

c. Harmony came from discord.

d. Life came from nonlife.

e. Reason came from irrationality.

f. Personality came from nonpersonality.

g. Morality came from amorality.

Believing the above claims of the materialist takes far greater faith than believing that a personal, infinite, rational God created this universe!

4. *Materialism does not correspond to reality.*[15]

The world appears to be more than matter, so materialism

---

[14]William Edward Lammerts, ed., *Scientific Studies in Creation* (Phillipsburg, N.J.: Presbyterian and Reformed Publishing Co., 1971).

[15]Bernard Ramm, *Protestant Christian Evidences* (Chicago: Moody Press, 1966), pp. 59, 60.

simply denies what it cannot explain. Simple denials carry very little weight with the thinking person. If all is matter, then where did the idea of "mind" come from? If all is matter, then why and how do we account for mental/emotional phenomena such as intention and memory? Why are the materialists kept busy trying to explain away the experiences of people who have had contact with the supernormal or supernatural?

5. *The findings of modern physicists, particularly in the field of quantum mechanics and Heisenberg's principle of indeterminacy, have raised serious doubts about the scientific validity of materialism's understanding of the nature of reality.*[16]

Many young physicists lean toward Eastern idealism, which assumes reality to be "mind," and denies the existence of "matter"! There is a growing fascination with Taoism or Buddhism as a religious framework for modern physics.[17] Why? The sterile character of Western materialism has driven people into the seductive arms of Eastern mysticism. The pendulum has begun to swing from the extreme of materialism to the extreme of idealism.

Dr. Bernard Ramm foretold this shift toward idealism in modern physics in 1953. His prophetic words are worth considering:

> Both Nevius and Hocking believe that the current shift in physics from the older Newtonian physics to the new relativity and atomic physics is seriously damaging to the naturalistic program. . . . If the contentions of such men as H. Weyl, A. Compton, J. Jeans, W. Carr, A. Eddington, and F. Northrop are correct, then it is conceivable that fifty years of science will see an abandonment of the naturalistic program by the scientists. . . . The slight breeze in the direction of idealism may turn to prevailing winds.[18]

People familiar with modern physics know there is a growing movement toward idealism which is fearless and aggressive. Materialism is vulnerable, because as an attempt to ex-

---

[16]Michael Cosgrove, *The Essence of Man* (Grand Rapids: Zondervan, 1977), p. 34.

[17]Gary Zukav, *The Dancing Wu Li Masters: An Overview of the New Physics* (New York: Bantam Books, 1979).

[18]Ramm, *Protestant Christian Evidences*, p. 58.

plain the world, it is beset by a simplistic and reductionistic methodology which renders it philosophically unacceptable.

Materialism and Man

We now come to the most difficult part of the theory of materialism. Its adherents believe man is only an electrochemical machine, that everything man is and does can be explained solely in terms of the movement of particles of matter. Man does not have a mind, self, or soul which is different or distinct from his body, particularly his brain. Qualitatively speaking, man is no different than bricks or bats. He has nothing more, and is no greater, than any other material object.

Is this view of man true? Does it satisfy the demands of reason and human experience? What are the implications for society if it is true?

1. Materialism is once again guilty of reductionism.
Mark Cosgrove explains:

> Reductionism is a way of viewing man that reduces him to an explanation of his parts, i.e., man equals a collection of individual brain and body processes. But reductionism is unable to answer why the whole man seems to be more than the sum of his physical parts.[19]

If the materialistic theory is true, a man and a rock are exactly the same. Neither man nor rock possesses "mind" or "soul"; both are simply a collection of atoms. If this is so, then materialists should easily explain why rocks do not think, feel and make decisions, yet man does these things. Or, since materialism views man as being qualitatively equal to animals, its adherents also should easily explain why animals do not experience self-awareness, religious worship, aesthetic feelings, and moral emotions. The materialists have yet to explain why and how man does what rocks or animals cannot do.

We must conclude that man cannot artificially be reduced to a random collection of atoms and be placed in the same category as rocks or dogs, though the materialists reduce man

---

[19]Cosgrove, *The Essence of Man*, p. 28.

to that category simply by denying all those things which distinquish man from the rest of the creation. This is clearly understood by materialist scholars, such as B. F. Skinner, who stated in *Beyond Freedom and Dignity*, "To man Qua man we readily say good riddance" (p. 200).

2. *Materialism cannot adequately explain man.*

A philosophy must adequately explain reality as it is perceived by man. Materialism, however, does not correspond to what man is or does.

a. Materialism has never successfully refuted Descartes' argument for the existence of "self." To doubt or deny the existence of "self" really proves its existence, because the activity of doubt demands the existence of the doubter. Materialists are like the man who searched his house and, finding no one, declared, "No one is at home." Or again, they are like the child who, when asked, "Is anyone home?" replied, "No one is here." Man's self-awareness is intuitive and necessary to thought itself. To deny it is to prove it.

b. Materialism has never developed a plausible theory for the origin or survival of man's morality, aesthetic appreciation, religious drive, rationality, personality, pride, sense of responsibility, and self-awareness. In his classic, *The Foundations of Belief,* Arthur James Balfour argues that, given the materialists' evolutionary premise of the survival of the fittest, man's ethics, aesthetics, and reason should have been bred out of humanity long ago.[20] The materialists have never explained why or how man enjoys good music or a beautiful sunset. Neither can they explain why or how aesthetic feelings fit into a materialistic world. Rocks and cats do not appreciate the beauties of art or of this world.

Balfour applies this same argument to ethics and reason. If materialism is true, such things should not exist. Since they do, materialism is erroneous. And since the denial of the consequence is always valid in logic, Balfour's argument has never been answered.

Materialism fails to deal with the evidence that reason tran-

---

[20]Balfour, *The Foundations of Belief,* pp. 4–86.

scends neurology, morality transcends stimulus, memory transcends time, and freedom transcends causality.[21] In fact, by assuming their theory is true, the materialists refuse to reduce it to a "secretion" born out of the random motion of nonrational atoms. They assume their reason transcends neurology.

If stimulus is the source of morality, then the self-gratification of the pleasure zones of the brain would be the basis of ethics. But ethics is based on universal principles which call upon man to deny self-gratification for the good of others. Hence, morality transcends stimulus.

The fact that man remembers the past, perceives the present, and anticipates the future reveals that he is a transcendent self as well as a body. People with major brain damage still have a transcendence above time in which they talk about the past, present, and future. Seeing that the past no longer exists and the future has not arrived, if thoughts are the result of the present motion of nonrational atoms, how and why does man remember the past and anticipate the future? Since there is no "past" or "future" stimulating the brain, from whence does memory or anticipation come?

If man is a machine, then all of his thoughts, words and deeds are predictable and capable of being conditioned. Since we can condition a dog to salivate at the ring of a bell, if materialism is true, we can train all men to secrete the thoughts of materialism at the ring of a bell. But man is not predictable and cannot be totally conditioned.

If mechanistic conditioning were possible, how can the resistance by such men as Solzhenitsyn to Soviet conditioning be explained? The millions of people suffering in Communist concentration camps reveal the failure of the materialists to condition people, even when the materialists have unlimited political power and the use of all forms of conditioning from drugs to torture. By their failure, the Soviet materialists have demonstrated that man is unpredictable and cannot be programmed like a computer or conditioned like a dog. Man's freedom transcends causality.

---

[21]Ramm, *Protestant Christian Evidences*, pp. 61–70.

3. *Materialism's simplistic identification of man's mind as his brain does not correspond to the findings of modern brain research.* Human intuition has always resisted identifying "mind" or "self" with some part of the body. People have an intrinsic awareness that while the "self" has a body, the "self" is not the body. A man can lose his hand or foot in an accident and yet feel no loss of "self." One Vietnam veteran who had lost both arms and legs stated that he did not feel his "self," "ego," or "soul" was in any way affected by the loss of bodily parts. The "self" or "mind" cannot be identified as the body or simply some process of the body.

Realizing that the loss of body parts does not affect man's awareness of his "self" or "mind," modern materialists have selected only one part of the body to be identified as the "self," "mind," or "ego." They chose the organ we call the brain. They assumed that "mind" was simply a descriptive word for how the brain worked. Thus, the mind did not exist in some nonmaterial way; it was only the result of the random motion of nonrational atoms in the brain. The mind and the brain were one. What one did, the other did also.

The materialists committed a major anatomical error when they identified the mind as the brain. They failed to see that man's "mind" or "self" is in the brain much as a hand may be in a glove. William James compared the relationship of the mind to the brain by the analogy of light shining through a prism.[22] To identify the light as the prism or the mind as the brain is nonsense.

A pioneer of modern brain research, Sir Charles Sherrington, started out believing materialism's identification of the mind as the brain. As a result of his lifelong research on the brain, however, he concluded in *Man on His Nature* (Cambridge University Press, 1963) that it was an error to equate the mind with the brain. After years of research he declared: "That our being should consist of two fundamental elements offers, I suppose, no greater inherent improbability than that

---

[22]Gilson, Langin and Maurer, *Recent Philosophy* (New York: Random House, 1966), p. 678.

it should rest on one only."[23] After conducting brain research in connection with epilepsy, prominent Canadian neurosurgeon Wilder Penfield provided startling evidence that the mind is not the brain. Penfield discovered that the mind is not a computer, but has a computer—the brain. The mind of man is related to the brain as a computer programmer is related to a computer, or as a viewer is related to the TV he is watching. Thus, man has a mind and a brain.

What evidence led Penfield and others to reject the materialists' identification of the mind as the brain? A large body of evidence has been collected by Penfield in *The Mystery of the Mind*, and by Popper and Eccles in *The Self and Its Brain*.[24] Perhaps one example from their books would help at this point.

While under a local anesthetic, an epileptic's scalp was lifted away, and the cranium opened to allow the surgeon direct access to the brain tissue. Using an electrical probe, he touched that part of the brain which made the right hand move or twitch. As the hand moved, he said to the patient, "You just moved your hand." The patient replied, "I didn't move it, you did." Evidently, the man's self-awareness was not directly related to his brain.

The surgeon then directed the patient to will in his mind not to let his right hand move. The patient agreed to resist moving it in his mind and as the hand began to twitch due to the application of the electric probe, the patient's left hand reached over and stopped the right hand from moving. The physician could control the brain and make it move the right hand, but the mind of the patient, which transcended the brain, moved the left hand to stop it! If the patient's mind and brain were identical, then the surgeon would have been able to control the patient's mind as well as his brain. In reality, the patient's mind was free from the physician's manipulation of the brain.

The materialists' identification of the mind as the brain

---

[23]Quoted by Arthur Custance in Wilder Penfield et al., *The Mystery of the Mind*, (Princeton, N.J.: Princeton University Press, 1975), p. 55.
[24]See: Wilder Penfield, *The Mystery of The Mind*, ibid.; K.R. Popper and J.C. Eccles, *The Self and Its Brain* (New York: Springer-Verlag, 1977).

may have seemed plausible in the nineteenth century when brain research was in its primal stage, but it simply cannot stand up to modern brain research. Cosgrove comments, "A simple materialistic explanation for all that man is and does will not fit with human experience or with what we know about the human brain."[25]

4. Materialists cannot live what they believe.

Materialists cannot logically believe in "love," yet they fall in love and marry. They cannot believe in "mind," yet they cannot avoid using "mind" terminology in their speech when referring to themselves or others. They believe that man is a random swarm of nonrational atoms no different than stones, yet they value people and relationships—they do not treat their children or mates as random atoms. What they say in the classroom is therefore contradicted by how they live in the home. They experience the mystery and beauty of this world and man while denying that such things exist.

Materialism is not a faith to live by or die by. It is unlivable because it is merely a philosophy of negation, denying anything that is worth living or dying for.

5. Materialism leads to the denial of all the social values and ethics which have formed the basis of human worth, freedom and democracy.

Materialists, from the left or the right, are committed to destroying the freedom and worth of man. The world they envision was prophetically portrayed in Orwell's *1984* and graphically described in Solzhenitsyn's *Gulag Archipelago*. It is a frightening world of oppression and terror in which an elite group attempts to control the masses by torture, drugs, and other manipulations. In effect, the whole world becomes one vast Nazi concentration camp. One can almost smell the smoke of the ovens as one reads Skinner's *Beyond Freedom and Dignity*. No wonder C. S. Lewis entitled his analysis of materialism's view of man as *The Abolition of Man*. Our generation will do well to heed Francis Schaeffer's observation in *Back to Freedom and Dignity*:

---

[25]Cosgrove, *The Essence of Man*, p. 25.

If we follow Skinner, we are left with a total skepticism in regard to all knowledge and knowing. Further, if the only way man is able to function in either knowledge or values is as Skinner does by acting on the basis of that which he and his system destroy, are we not left with Skinner himself as a pitiful man—not as a rat or a pigeon pushing levers but as a poor, optimistic rat or pigeon pushing levers.[26]

Conclusion

As a world view, materialism is neither philosophically nor logically valid because it carries within itself the seeds of its own destruction. It does not correspond to what the world is. It does not describe man as he is or does. It is unlivable on a personal level and unbearable on a political level. Materialism is thus a rotted pillar which cannot give any support to modern atheism. It has failed the tests of reason and experience.

[26]Francis Schaeffer, *Back To Freedom and Dignity* (Chicago: InterVarsity Press, 1973), p. 73.

9

A Sample Debate

The following transcript was taken from a debate between myself and a woman named Sheila, a representative of the Freedom From Religion Foundation. An avowed atheist, Sheila claimed she could disprove the existence of God, the truthfulness of the Bible, and the historical existence of Christ.

Actually I had hoped to debate the woman who was the founder and head of the Freedom From Religion Foundation. I had heard her on a Philadelphia radio talk show, during which she claimed the Bible supports rape, murder, incest, cannibalism, and other abominable acts. Most of her statements were so outlandish that we agreed she or one of her representatives would debate the issues on my Chicago program. We would have ninety minutes on a secular AM station (which reached three states) during prime time on a weekday afternoon.

I have excised from the full transcript commercials, news briefs, weather forecasts and other interruptions which had nothing to do with the debate. Also, I have edited portions of the transcript in which the speaker lost sight of grammar and syntax in the heat of the moment, or mispronounced words. Punctuation proved to be more difficult than imagined, but utmost care has been taken to render a transcript as accurate and readable as possible. (A cassette recording of the debate is available for $3.50 from the Research and Education Foundation, R.D. #2, Box 161, Millerstown, PA 17062.)

The moderator, Al Mann, tried to give each side equal time to present its position. His masterful skill in this difficult role contributed much to the success of the debate. The transcript opens with Mann's request for Sheila to give her opening statement.

The Debate

Sheila: This is a subject that I have been absolutely fascinated with for the past eight months. The Freedom From Religion Foundation went on television with a program, *Jesus: Man, Myth, or Fraud*, and it was at that time I decided I'd better learn something about the historicity of Jesus.

When I started digging into it, I found out that the overwhelming number of Protestant biblical scholars today do not believe that Jesus of Nazareth, that a Jesus in other words who said and did all of the things that the gospels say that he said and did, probably, in their view, never existed. And, that if there was any kind of a Jesus upon whom Christianity is founded, that type of Jesus we really know nothing about. And this is what I have been consuming myself with the last eight months—studying the historicity of Jesus. And I am absolutely positive that there was not a Jesus of Nazareth any more than there was a Paul Bunyan.

Morey: Well, I think she gave the answer when she mentioned that she's been looking at it out of curiosity for about eight months. I myself have looked at the primary sources for over twenty years.

The historicity of Jesus is founded upon more historical evidence than what is needed for any other historical character. If anyone looks at the primary documentation from Roman sources and Jewish sources such as the Talmud and the Mishnah, you can get ten, twenty, thirty, forty literary references to Jesus of Nazareth in the first century, many of them before A.D. 70.

Even the enemies of Christ, such as the Jewish writers who wrote against Jesus in the Talmud, or the heathen or pagan writers, did not deny the existence of Jesus. They would be the counterpart of Sheila in the early part of the Church. All of them, without hesitation, admitted that Jesus lived and they admitted that he taught and what he did.

Sheila's basic error has been pointed out by John Montgomery in his book, *History and Christianity*. What he points out is that there are modern anti-Christian thinkers, particularly in Germany, who, because they are rationalists, have simply said, "Reality will correspond to what I think it is. Don't confuse me with the archaeological facts. My mind is already made up."

When the *New York Times* pointed out that a portion of the Gospel of Luke was found, which must be dated A.D. 57, and possibly a piece of Mark, which may be dated A.D. 50 (now, we're talking about the Gospel of Luke probably being written within twenty years after the death of Christ), the same modern theologians said, "We cannot accept the archaeological finds because it would destroy our theory." Even the *New York Times* couldn't resist saying these are examples of people who simply do not want the primary sources and the facts to destroy their theories.

Mann: All right, Sheila, Dr. Morey has made a couple of points. First of all, he refers to primary documentation. He says there is more evidence than is necessary to establish the identity of any historical figure. What kind of information have you found? What is the basis of your conclusion?

Sheila: He's absolutely incorrect. There is no real evidence that Jesus of Nazareth existed and there is all kinds of evidence that he did not. The books that I have read were written by men who have spent their lifetime studying this. This isn't just me and my little eight months. This is the writing of people who have spent their entire life on it, and he will find out that if you look at the writings of Paul.

Paul is the only historical writer. And Paul did not give a historical account of Jesus of Nazareth in Acts. And Paul's Jesus is a completely different Jesus than you find in the Gospels. There's no comparison whatsoever. Paul's Jesus does not do any miracles. The Gospels' Jesus is absolutely full of miracles all over the place. Paul's Jesus doesn't give any huge teachings on ethics. Paul's Jesus was not killed by the Jews. The Gospel writers absolutely loved to blame the killing of Jesus on the Jews. Paul, in his writings, does not mention who Jesus' parents were. He does not say where this Jesus supposedly was killed. He tells us absolutely nothing about this guy, who supposedly he was a greatest admirer or follower of. We know nothing about a Jesus from Paul's writings.

Mann: All right, let's take this matter of Paul. What was the purpose of Paul's writings?

Sheila: Paul was hung up on this risen Christ. G. A. Wells seems to think that where it all came from was the Jewish wisdom literature—an idea that a Messiah would come, probably a son of David, because David was the Jews' most successful king. And when a flesh and blood one didn't come, then this king had to come from heaven. That this Messiah would come comes right out of the Jewish Wisdom literature.

And the Jesus of the Jewish Wisdom literature is not the Jesus of the Gospels. He's totally a different person. Also, Paul never called Jesus, "Jesus of Nazareth" or "the Son of Man."

By the way, there is no evidence whatsoever that there was a city or a place called the city of Nazareth in the first century. You do not find a place called the city of Nazareth in the Old Testament, in the Talmud, or in Josephus' writings. And, if you want to get into the Gospels, the Gospels are not historical documents.

Mann: Dr. Morey, Sheila says that Paul was the only historical writer in the New Testament. Is that your understanding? And also, that his Jesus was an entirely different

Jesus than the Jesus of the other Gospel writers.

Morey: Well, it would come as quite a shock to the Apostle Paul. He quotes from the Gospel of Luke in such places as 1 Timothy 5. He was familiar with the Gospels. They were written before he wrote his Epistles. There was no reason for him to give a biography when there were four of them already in circulation.

As I have already stated, the evidence of the historicity of Jesus relies first on the New Testament. And we have portions of it found in the Dead Sea Scrolls which can be dated A.D. 50, 57, 66, etc.

You also have the Jewish sources: the Talmud which says that Jesus was the bastard son of Mary and a Roman soldier and even gives his name; the Mishnah which says that all followers of this Jesus will suffer eternal punishment; some of the Jewish apocalyptic literature which attacks those who followed Jesus. Also, there are Roman historians and Josephus.

Mann: All right, now what about Josephus?

Sheila: We have a difference of opinion with absolutely everything that this guy is saying. I can't believe him! Paul is the only historical writer and Paul wrote before the Gospels were even written. Paul is the closest one to this supposedly Jesus character. The other writings were after this. That's why Paul's Jesus is different than the Gospels' Jesus—because he didn't have the Gospels.

Mann: All right, Dr. Morey, Sheila suggests that Paul's writings came before the writings of all the other people who wrote the books of the New Testament.

Morey: Well—

Sheila: That's right. Now, the Dead Sea Scrolls don't even mention a Jesus. The Dead Sea Scrolls have to do with a teacher of righteousness and it's possible that this Jesus idea, I mean there are a lot of ideas, but one of the possibilities is that Jesus was built around this "teacher of righteousness" of the Dead Sea Scrolls.

Josephus! Every honest theologian today knows

that the long passage in Josephus is an interpolation. It's been known to be an interpolation since 1838 when Nathaniel Lardner first debated it in a book called *Jewish Testimony*, volume six, of the works published in London. I don't even need this guy to tell me that!

Mann: All right, Dr. Morey. What about Josephus and what about the matter of the order of the Gospels? When did Paul write his Epistles?

Morey: If you would have been keeping up with reports in *Newsweek, Time, New York Times, London Times, Biblical Archaeological Review*, etc., you would have read that there has come a drastic shift. Dr. John A. T. Robinson has thoroughly now discredited the idea of dating the Gospels after A.D. 70.[1] In the Dead Sea Scrolls there were found portions of the New Testament. For example, the Gospel of Mark. Part of that has to be dated around A.D. 50. Or, Luke dated A.D. 57. Or, a part of the Acts from A.D. 66.[2]

These things are physically sitting there. This has been reported by the media. And this immediately discredits all the nineteenth-century theologians which Sheila is depending upon.

Besides Josephus, which I believe is a valid reading and there are good scholars for that, you also have passages in Tacitus, Suetonius, Lucian, Thallus, Serapion, etc.[3] Now, since you have never dealt with the

---

[1]John A. T. Robinson, *Redating the New Testament* (Philadelphia: Westminster Press, 1976).

[2]David Estrada and William White, Jr., *The First New Testament* (Nashville: Thomas Nelson, 1978).

[3]See: Norman Anderson, *Jesus Christ: The Witness of History* (Downer's Grove, Ill.: InterVarsity Press, 1985).

E.M. Blaiklock, *Jesus Christ: Man or Myth?* (Nashville: Thomas Nelson, 1974).

F.F. Bruce, *Jesus and Christian Origins Outside the New Testament* (Grand Rapids: Eerdmans, 1974).

I. Howard Marshall, *I Believe in the Historical Jesus* (Grand Rapids: Eerdmans, 1977).

Josh McDowell, *Evidence That Demands a Verdict* (San Bernardino, Cal.: Campus Crusade, 1972).

primary resources, have you read Tacitus?[4]

Sheila: Tacitus wrote his annals around 120 A.D. There is nothing written by the Christians, the Jews, or the pagans before the end of the first century; and by the time the second century rolled around, the Jewish writers were already believing that this legend that the Christians told them. Besides, I've read what it—

Mann: Let's give Dr. Morey a chance to answer.

Morey: Suetonius mentions that in A.D. 49 the Jews were expelled from Rome under Claudius because riots had broken out as they were fighting over the issue of whether or not Jesus was the Christ.

We also have, in A.D. 74, a pagan philosopher writing a letter who mentions Jesus. Mara is his name. This letter has been translated. It's not anything I have dug up myself. It's in the Ante-Nicene fathers where he compares Jesus of Nazareth to such people as Socrates.[5]

We also have the Nazareth Stone, A.D. 50. It is an archaeological fact. You are ignorant of this because you don't deal with the primary resources.

You are dealing with thinkers who were either nineteenth-century critics or people who today rely upon them. For example, the foolishness of the "Paul *vs.* Jesus" business was refuted by Dr. Gresham Machen at Princeton Seminary.[6] It has been thoroughly discredited and it's only those who hearken back to the old nineteenth-century German rationalists who pay any attention to it whatsoever.

---

[4]Cornelius Tacitus (A.D. c. 55–A.D. c. 117) referred to Christians and their Christ in his *Annals* (XV.44) and in his *Histories* (Sulpicius Severus Chron. ii. 30.6). His statement about Christ is dated as around A.D. 112, not 120.

[5]*The Ante-Nicene Fathers* (Grand Rapids: Eerdmans, 1981), Vol. VIII, pp. 735f.

[6]See: Gresham Machen, *The Origin of Paul's Religion* (Grand Rapids: Eerdmans, 1925).

Herman Ridderbos, *Paul and Jesus* (Philadelphia: Presbyterian and Reformed Publishing Co., 1958).

Seyoon Kim, *The Origin of Paul's Gospel* (Grand Rapids: Eerdmans, 1981).

Mann: Sheila, you made a point and I wanted to get a clari-
fication from you on that. Do you believe that because
each of the forty some writers of the sixty-six books of
the Bible don't rehash what each other said, that means
that some are more reliable than others?

Sheila: Well, no. It's just that you have to look at it from a
point of history. And, for sure, Paul is a historical writer.
But what they do is they compare these different books
in the Bible and then they compare to reliable history
from the historians that were writing at that time. And,
by looking at them, and the things that the Gospel
writers wrote, you can tell if they're historical or not.

This guy, I can't believe him! He mentioned something about this disturbance going on in Rome in 49
A.D. For crying out loud, even the New Testament
doesn't claim that Jesus was alive and in Rome in 49
A.D.

I want to get back to Josephus because Josephus
never wrote about a Jesus. Those two statements are
obvious interpolations and anybody with any common sense can figure it out for themselves. It's thought
that Eusebius—well, at least Eusebius is the number
one suspect for this fraudulent interpolation because
before Eusebius's time, none of these Christians
pointed to that passage and said, "Hey, here's proof
that Jesus lived." And Eusebius did brag about being
able to lie for the Church and it was okay to lie for the
Church!

How come that Josephus does not say that there
was a Jesus who died under Pilate? How come Josephus, an Orthodox Jew, doesn't write about this mad-
man running into the temple—private property, mind
you—swinging his sword and chasing out the traitors?
How come Josephus doesn't write about the time when
Jesus was born, when all these little babies are supposed to be killed? How come Josephus doesn't write
about that?

Mann: All right, let's direct those specific questions to Dr.
Morey.

Morey: First of all, let me clarify something. As I stated, in the Dead Sea Scrolls, it was reported in all the mass media in 1972 that parts of the New Testament had been found and dated.

I'm now going to quote from the *New York Times*: "St. Mark, written only a few years after the death of Jesus."

Or, what about the *Chicago Tribune*: "If this is accepted, biblical research will be revolutionized."

Listen to the *Los Angeles Times*: "Nine New Testament fragments dated A.D. 50 to A.D. 100 have been discovered in a Dead Sea cave."

Mann: So what does that prove? What is your point by these quotations?

Morey: Number one, you have written descriptions of the life of Jesus written within ten years of His death within in the generation of those living who, if these Gospels were fabrications, the enemies of Christianity such as the Jewish writers in the Talmud, etc., could have and would have said Jesus never existed.

The enemies of Christianity in the first, second and third centuries never said that Jesus didn't live and that Jesus did not do what He did. What they said was that either He was an Egyptian magician, as the pagans claim, or that He was a demon-possessed man, as some Jewish writers claim.

The Gospels must be dated early. *Time* magazine in 1977 pointed this out. The March 21, 1977, edition, for your sake, Sheila. So, you can look it up.

This woman is depending upon what she calls "common sense." As a theologian, as a historian, I don't depend upon "common sense," but upon documentation and historical research.

Mann: Sheila, what have you got against using books as a source of history, written within ten years of the death of the subject of the books?

Sheila: I have nothing against the books that he depends upon when they actually were written. This guy seems to think that the Dead Sea Scrolls contain portions of

Mark and Matthew. For crying out loud, the Dead Sea Scrolls were many, many years B.C.!

This "Teacher of Righteousness," they seem to think, died probably somewhere in 60 B.C. How in the world could the Gospel of Mark, which he told us was supposedly already in bits and pieces around 35, 37 A.D., be contained in a book that was written way before that?

And, besides, it doesn't make any difference if this particular book was supposedly written sooner. The fact of the matter is, we do know that when Paul wrote—and Paul has a totally different Jesus than the Jesus portrayed in the Gospels—and Paul, in his youth, should have known this character if He lived at this time and we would know something about Him.

Mann: Doesn't Paul quote the other Gospels?

Sheila: There are only eight books—no, seven books that Paul actually wrote. There are many that are attributed to Paul that he never wrote. The four absolute ones are 1 and 2 Corinthians, Galatians, and Romans, and there are some other ones he possibly wrote. But there are things attributed to him that he never wrote.

The thing is, you have a different Jesus and not only do you have a different Jesus between Paul's Jesus and the Gospel's, you have all kinds of different Jesuses in the Gospels. And this is what makes the Gospels so terribly contradictory.

Mann: Now, what do you mean, "different kinds of Jesuses"?

Sheila: I'll tell you what. I can't stand these ministers today. You get on a show, and you say, "Okay, Jesus said— this character said, 'I came not to bring peace but a sword and ye that hath no sword let him sell his garment and buy one and bring my enemies before me and slay them.' " And then, they'll turn around and say Jesus said that, "They that take the sword shall perish with the sword and blessed are the peacemakers."

You see, you have a Jesus who is a hawk and a

Jesus who is a dove. Now you have these total con-
tradictions and the reason you have these contradic-
tions is because of the characters who wrote Matthew,
Mark, Luke, and John. And nobody knows who wrote
Matthew, Mark, Luke, and John! Matthew did not write
Matthew. Luke did not write Luke. Mark did not write
Mark. These were titles that were assigned to the Gos-
pels some time during the second century.

Now when these evangelists put words into the
mouth of their Jesus that came through tradition, they
believed that He said them. This is the reason you
come up with all these contradictions in the Bible.

Mann: All right, now we've got a lot of points here—contradictions in the Bible, different Jesuses, etc. But let's
start back at your first comment and ask Dr. Morey.
Sheila says that the Dead Sea Scrolls were written before any of the people who wrote the Gospels. So, how
could they refer to anything in the Gospels?

Morey: Here again, she shows her ignorance of the field of
Dead Sea Scroll research. I've been to Israel and examined the Isaiah scroll. The Dead Sea Scrolls have a
lot of material from the first century as well as from
B.C. or before the birth of Christ.

As I have stated, particularly in the book, *The First
New Testament*, by Dr. Estrada and Dr. White, modern
theologians and those involved in textual criticism and
archaeology, without hesitation, are now seeing that
portions of the New Testament were found in one of
the caves in the Dead Sea area. That is the fact. They're
sitting there.

Mann: Okay, let's stick with the Dead Sea Scrolls. Sheila is
going to argue that they were written before Christ
and you're going to argue that they contain information after the death of Christ.

Morey: They contain information about the Essenic community. They also contain information about some of the
revolts that went on in the first century.

Mann: Okay. I don't think we can resolve this any further. So, let's go on to something else—the different Jesuses contained in the Gospels. How would you respond when she says that Paul's Jesus is different than any of the Jesuses of the other Gospel writers?

Morey: Well, I would say that again, she's a lay person who's never studied the original languages. She probably doesn't have a degree in history or theology or philosophy. She spent eight months taking a brief look at this issue. It's clear that she's only read people who would give her what she wants to hear. She is taking verses out of context. This is the old game that the rationalists have always played: "Don't confuse me with the archaeological facts. Let me spend my theories in freedom."

I would just like to challenge Sheila to read the documentation found in the primary sources. Don't depend upon modern rationalists who've already made up their mind that they don't want to believe in Jesus Christ and to face the evidence that is there. The evidence is in the Talmud. It's in the early Church Fathers. It's in the Roman historians and in letters. It's there archaeologically in the Nazareth Stone and in the grave inscriptions of the first century. There are Christian grave inscriptions from the first century. The evidence is there.

Mann: All right, a couple more things that Sheila said, and then we can go on. What's this thing about the different Jesuses of the Gospel writers?

Morey: A fabrication of her own mind. She is taking verses out of context.

Mann: All right, let's take this hawk vs. dove contradiction—or apparent contradiction.

Morey: When Jesus said, "I have come to bring not peace, but a sword," if you look at the context, He's talking about divisions within a family. I just talked recently with Madalyn Murray O'Hair's son. Now that he has become a Christian, his mother, being an atheist, has severed all relationships with him. Well, this is exactly the context Jesus was talking about. Some people will sever their relationship with you because of your allegiance to God and that is the context in Matthew 10.

    Christ was not saying I have come to bring a literal sword to go and cut people's heads off. He was talking in the context of the fact that a personal relationship to Him would mean that some people wouldn't be able to accept it. They would seek to stop you.

Sheila: That's correct. I know that. But, at the same time, you don't understand that you have this Jesus coming to divide up families. So much for your Christian family life—great guy that He was!

Morey: That wasn't a Christian family that He's dividing. Since it was Madalyn O'Hair who rejected her son and will not even answer his letters, whose fault is that? That is not Christ's problem; that's Madalyn's problem.

Sheila: It happens to be neither Christ's or Madalyn's problem because there is no one by the name of Christ because Christ is not a name. It is a title that means "Anointed One." There were other Christs throughout history; there were other Messiahs throughout history. All it means is "anointed," and if you want to read the Bible literally, the Jesus of the Gospels wasn't even anointed.

Mann: That's a good point. Dr. Morey, let's go back and forth here with brief comments and then we can get responses from both of you. She said that Jesus was not anointed.

Morey: This—

Sheila: He knows he wasn't. Elijah was supposed to come back from the dead and anoint the Messiah. Elijah never made it.

Morey: Number one, you don't even know what the word *Christos* means. Yes, the derivation or the etymology of the word had to do with anointing. But by the time the New Testament was written and Jesus came on the scene, it meant Messiah. He was anointed by the Holy Spirit at His baptism. This is the whole theme of

Matthew 3. He was anointed by the Holy Spirit, says Matthew, says John. He was the Anointed One of God, the Christ.

Sheila: That's what the Christians made up! But the prophecy of the Old Testament was that He was actually supposed to be literally anointed. So, what does your Jesus of the Gospels do? He goes and tries to make the people think that John the Baptist was Elijah and, of course, John the Baptist says he wasn't. But then Christians wrote the Gospels, so they could put in John the Baptist's mouth whatever they wanted.

Morey: There is no verse in the Old Testament which says that He, i.e., the Messiah, would be literally anointed. Give me the reference right here and now.

Sheila: I'm supposed to remember every passage in the Bible, word for word?

Morey: No, but you shouldn't use a verse if you don't have any documentation.

Sheila: If you gave me time to look it up, I would. But it would probably take me a while. That book's a big book. For crying out loud, I wouldn't say it if it wasn't true!

Mann: Let's go to one other thing that's already been mentioned. We should talk about Josephus. Then we can go on to new things. But let's try to cover what we've already talked about.

Dr. Morey, Sheila asked some questions about why this historian did not include all of these important points that she enumerated, if indeed he was writing about the Jesus that you're talking about.

Morey: I—

Sheila: How's come he doesn't write about the slaughter of the innocents and this Jesus running in and swinging His whip in the temple? And how's come He doesn't write about all these zombies who allegedly arose from their graves when Jesus arose? Don't you think that if that happened Josephus would have written about it? He doesn't write about any of these wild tales.

Mann: All right, Dr. Morey.

Morey: Number one, let's clarify some things about Josephus. Every manuscript ever found has in it the statements concerning John the Baptist, the death of James the Apostle, who is called the "brother of the Lord," and the life of Jesus, who was called the Christ. Every single manuscript.

Mann: What manuscripts?

Morey: The manuscripts we can pick up and touch, going back over a thousand years in several different languages.

Mann: What manuscripts?

Morey: The manuscripts of Josephus' book on the Jewish Wars. They are quoted by other Church Fathers and not just Eusebius. It's also quoted by pagan writers who were against Christianity. This means that the passage in Josephus was not an interpolation or stuck in there by somebody. Where is the physical proof that it was an interpolation? There isn't any.

Number two, nearly all of Sheila's arguments are, in logic, called an argument from silence which is invalid. The purpose of Josephus was not to write a biography of Jesus. He mentions Jesus, John the Baptist, James the Apostle—the brother of the Lord, and he mentions other people. His purpose is not a biography of Christ.

I have read through the works of Josephus, so, I have a question for Sheila—yes or no. Have you read through the works of Josephus—yes or no?

Sheila: You know that I haven't. But, at the same time, you are believing what you know ain't so. For crying out loud, that's what Mark Twain said. You're believing it on faith. You're taking that leap of faith.

If you look at that passage in Josephus, what kind of an Orthodox Jew—and Josephus said that he was— would have said this is the Christ? (Which is how that is interpreted.) And how come this passage is taken out of context and why does he say it has no meaning whatsoever that Josephus didn't tell you these other things?

Well, if Josephus took down every dirty little rotten thing that Herod ever did, and he did take down the dirty little rotten things that Herod did, he certainly wouldn't have messed up on the point of all these little babies being killed, and all those zombies rising from the dead. Believe me, he wouldn't have messed up on that. And this guy says he doesn't believe in common sense! He just goes on history? Well!

Morey: Sheila, you're the one who has blind faith. I'm the one who has gravestone inscriptions, Dead Sea Scroll manuscripts, pagan and Roman historians, letters, etc. I'm the one who has the facts, Sheila.

You're the one who, by faith, believes in your heart that Jesus didn't exist. And you say to me, "Don't confuse me with the facts." You're the one who is taking a leap of faith into eternal darkness because you do not want to bow the knee to Jesus Christ.

Mann: All right, let me resolve this one point that Sheila made very positively and Dr. Morey has made the opposite point quite positively. Sheila says the Dead Sea Scrolls don't mention Jesus Christ. Dr. Morey, can you provide a document that she would perhaps accept as reasonable documentation that the Dead Sea Scrolls do mention Jesus Christ?

Morey: I would suggest that the book, *The First New Testament*, by Drs. Estrada and White, published by Thomas Nelson, Inc.

Mann: Do you have a document from that book that people in the general public will accept? Sheila says the Dead Sea Scrolls don't mention Jesus. You say they do. Is there a document in this book that we could accept that would be a legitimate documentation that both sides could accept that could prove one way or the other?

Morey: The book gives about 27 photographs of the manuscripts in question and gives a full discussion of their identity and how they were dated. Dr. William White, who is a friend of mine, has his doctorate in Hebrew from Dropsy College. He is one of the most recognized scholars when it comes to Greek and Hebrew.

Also, Dr. Edwin Yamuchi was one of the teams of scholars asked to work with the Dead Sea Scrolls. He would be more than willing to speak to anyone concerning this. The documentation is there. As I said, it was in *Time* magazine, *Newsweek*, etc.

Mann: Well, we're trying to establish for the people who are listening which person here is right. Sheila, what documentation would you expect?

Sheila: I would just ask every single person who is listening to go to their local library and dig out every book that they have on the Dead Sea Scrolls on the shelves, and they will find, by looking in every single one of them, that the Dead Sea Scrolls that are about this teacher of righteousness, not about Jesus the Christ.

I will not say Jesus Christ, because Christ is not a name. It is a title, like Attila the Hun, or John the Baptist. Jesus the Christ is not mentioned in the Dead Sea Scrolls.

Mann: All right, Dr. Morey, Sheila says that people can go to the library and they'll find out that the Dead Sea Scrolls don't have anything to say about Jesus. Where would you have them go to find the opposite?

Morey: They need to make sure that when they pick up that book on the Dead Sea Scrolls that it was not written before the contents of Cave 7 had been translated. So, when you have, starting in 1972, the news of this reaching the *New York Times*, the *Los Angeles Times*, the *London Times*, the whole scholarly world was electrified because portions of the Gospels, not Essenes' material, but portions of Mark, Luke, etc., were discovered in this cave.

Mann: All right, now this is documented in *Time*, and the *New York Times*, etc.?

Morey: I'll quote again. *Los Angeles Times*: "Nine New Testament fragments dated A.D. 50 to A.D. 100 have been discovered in a Dead Sea cave."

To any unbiased person, this should answer it. But, as I said, those who have already made up their mind will say that "Reality must correspond to what I think it is."

Mann: All right, Sheila, how do you respond to the article in the *Los Angeles Times*?

Sheila: Now that I think of it, I do remember reading something about that a long time ago. You see, it's before I was into this subject. And what he says is correct. But I do not have as biased an opinion as he does, for sure.

Mann: All right, then you can't say that the Dead Sea Scrolls don't mention Jesus?

Sheila: What's really called the Dead Sea Scrolls don't mention Jesus—but there are probably some writings. See, the Dead Sea Scrolls were these Essenes who were on the very fringes of Judaism and if there were still some Essenes around about 50 A.D., which is what he mentioned, these Essenes were at that time. Remember, all they had to do was find the Gospels and copy down the things that the Gospels had.

If the Gospels were already there, the Essenes could have believed what the Gospel writers had written and incorporated them into their writings. So, it's possible that there were more Essenes' writings as these people lived further on. But history progresses and people come up with new ideas so the Essenes of the first century would have a very different philosophy than the Essenes of B.C.—just like the first Christians were different from the Jews.

The first Christians accepted the God of Israel in the Old Testament and the idea of a Messiah. Then the Christians later on went and blamed the Jews for killing their Jesus. The whole concept changes, so I could see how this could be.

Morey: Again, I would say to any listener, they need to go to a bookstore or a library and pick up some books on the Dead Sea Scrolls by such scholars as Burroughs or

Fisher. All of them will simply tell you that the term "Dead Sea Scrolls" means loosely any of those writings and artifacts found in those caves along the Dead Sea area.

I have been there and visited that area to see the caves in question. It doesn't exclusively refer to the Essenes B.C. or A.D. It is a loose term referring to the finds in that area.

Mann: Dr. Morey, earlier in the program Sheila asked you why Jesus was called "Jesus of Nazareth," when there was no Nazareth. I believe basically that was her question.

Morey: Yes—

Sheila: I said there was no evidence that it existed. It was not mentioned in the Old Testament. It's not mentioned in the Talmud. And it's not mentioned in these writings as a place.

There was another religious cult, as I like to call them, called Nazarenes or Nazarites, and this is why we think that some, possibly some evangelists, thought maybe Jesus was a Nazarene. And, if he was a Nazarene, therefore He probably came from a place called Nazareth. This is how the title got put in there.

But Paul never called his Jesus, "Jesus of Nazareth." And remember, Paul never accused the Jews of killing Jesus. If Paul lived close to this time and was familiar with these Gospel writings, which Dr. Morey seems to think that he was, why do you think that he wouldn't have accused the Jews if the other gospel writers did?

Mann: All right, we'll get to that. I want to ask you a question before Dr. Morey answers my question. Would you accept Paul as an authority? Is he a good historical writer? You quote him favorably all the time or at least you've referred to things that he says as being reasonable and understandable to your way of thinking. Is he not a historical authority then?

Sheila: Oh, I quote Paul all the time because Paul is the only historical writer of the New Testament. He's the only one that we know for sure actually wrote what he wrote, although there are books in the Bible that are attributed to Paul that—

Mann: Well, then isn't he someone who could give us historical evidence of the existence of Jesus?

Sheila: No, he cannot give us historical evidence because he doesn't say when a Jesus lived or when a Jesus died. He does not write a biography on any Jesus. Why? Because his Jesus was based on tradition, not on a real person. And if a Jesus lived, you know when Paul was a youth and Paul was this great admirer and Paul admits he became a Christian around 35 A.D., don't you think he'd tell us something about this guy that he loved? Don't you think he would have quoted this Jesus? He never said, "Jesus said this," or "Jesus said that." Never.

Mann: Dr. Morey, first answer the issue of Nazareth.

Morey: My first response is this: Sheila is committing the typical logical error that most rationalists have committed down through the years. They used to say, "There is no evidence whatsoever for Hittites. Thus they did not exist." Or, "There's no evidence that there was any writing in Moses' day. Therefore we can assume that there was no writing in Moses' day." Well, archaeology has shown that writing went back beyond Abraham, that there were the Hittites, the Jebusites, and all the rest of the "ites." Arguments from silence are never valid.

    When it comes to the Nazareth question, we do have the Nazareth Stone which must be dated at least A.D. 50, and you do have other—

Mann: What is this stone that you have referred to several times?

Morey: This was discovered in Palestine and was translated in the 1930s, and any book dealing with the Bible and archaeology will mention the Nazareth Stone and its find concerning that period of time.[7]

Number one, there is archaeological evidence for Nazareth.

Number two, even if there were, at this moment, no other evidence than beyond the historical accounts of the Gospels, which are history (the Pauline Epistles are theology and the Gospels are history), that does not logically imply that the place didn't exist. This is a logical error that Sheila is making at that point.

Sheila: There is no logical error. A stone! Anybody can pick up a stone and call it anything that you want to call it! How's come the Old Testament doesn't name a place called Nazareth? Josephus doesn't mention a place called Nazareth, and the Talmud doesn't mention a place called Nazareth.

Mann: Okay, that's a good question, Dr. Morey.

Morey: Since Sheila has admitted that she's never read Josephus and I doubt that she's ever read the Talmud, I don't think she's in a position to be so dogmatic.

Sheila: It's just that the things that I'm telling you today are the findings from Protestant theologians, not from these so-called German rationalists. I'd like to have him call up Rudolph Bultmann and see what he has to say. He's probably the most famous biblical scholar.

Mann: What about him, Dr. Morey?

Morey: Bultmann is one of the typical German rationalist theologians whose methodology is no longer accepted in most seminaries. He's passé because he made up his mind ahead of time what he was going to find in the Gospels and then searched desperately for it. You have Karl Barth, you have Brunner, you have Bultmann, etc. I can list all sorts of names. I'm sure I've read much more of them than Sheila has read. But all of these people are anti-Christians.

---

[7]The stone, a marble slab inscribed with a decree of Claudius, was discovered in 1878, but its importance was first seen in 1932. It has since been regarded as final proof of the existence of Nazareth in the first century.

Mann: You made a point that she hadn't read the entire writings of Josephus, and the Talmud, so what point are you trying to make by that?

Morey: What I said was that, logically speaking, you cannot deny the existence of a town just because there does not happen to be any physical or literary evidence beyond the Bible.

I'll take Lystra as an example in the book of Acts. For many years, there was no archaeological evidence that there was such a town as Lystra or Derbe until Sir William Ramsey of Oxford University found it. He was an agnostic that didn't believe in Christ or the Scriptures. He searched for such cities to test the Bible and when he did, he discovered that Lystra, etc., did exist. He found the coins and the monuments and all of that stuff.

This means that just because you do not have, at this time, collaborating evidence as to the existence of this or that town in Scripture, that logically can mean nothing more than at this time you do not have any collaborating evidence.

Mann: Good point. And I don't think that can be argued. But what she said was that Nazareth is not mentioned in the writings of Josephus or the Talmud and you responded that she hadn't read all the writings of Josephus or the Talmud. Are you suggesting that Nazareth is mentioned?

Morey: Sheila is speaking very dogmatically. As I said, she's a lay person. She has no credentials or credence in this area. She's dabbling in this area and when she says Josephus never mentions Nazareth, I have to take it with a grain of salt. I will have to look it up and see for myself. As I—

Sheila: Tonight, you call Wolfhart Pannenburg and H. Chadwick and Arthur Drewer and E. Norton and Nathaniel Ardner and Lindemann and Evans and Werner and Thompson and Archibald Robertson and all of these other people. Call them—oh, some of them are dead.

I'm going on the basis of what many theologians who have spent their lifetime have found out. It's not what I think or what I believe.

Mann: Is it possible that Dr. Morey could give you the name of a prominent theologian that might take a different point of view? What if he took a different point of view and he was just as prominent as the ones you have mentioned? Would that in any way change your outlook?

Sheila: I'd have to read what he has to say. You see, what I did was, I didn't take these guys as far as when it came to the Bible things that when they said, "Paul didn't say this" or "Paul didn't say that," I didn't take their word for it. I went to the Bible and I went through all things that this terrible woman-hater Paul had said. I read all of his writings to find out, Did Paul say there was a Mary and a Joseph? Did Paul say that Jesus died under Pilate? That He died in Jerusalem? I didn't take anybody's word for it. I checked it out for myself and it wasn't there.

Mann: Dr. Morey, what is the significance of this lack of information in Paul?

Morey: You see, this is another example of the violation of the laws of logic. When you argue from silence, all you can obtain from that is silence. That Paul did not mention that Jesus was potty-trained cannot logically infer that He never experienced potty-training.

Paul did not feel any need to refer to Pilate because the Gospels already existed. He quotes the words of Jesus in 1 Timothy 5—he quotes the Gospel of Luke. He refers to the words of Christ in 1 Timothy 6. And—

Sheila: Paul did not write the Timothys! He did not write that!

Morey: Well, you see, you can state that, but it says in the first line that he wrote it. And—

Sheila: Of course it says that, because whoever wanted to attribute it to him did it. You mean you believe the Bible literally?

Mann: She seems to have difficulty understanding how any-body could believe the Bible literally. So, I guess on this point we have a problem continuing on the previous subject. Sheila says that Matthew didn't write Matthew, Mark didn't write Mark, and Paul didn't write all of Paul. Dr. Morey, thirty-five seconds.

Morey: That's her opinion. But seeing that she has never studied the primary sources, all she has is guesswork. I can ignore that. The evidence is fairly on the other side as argued by A. T. Robertson in his books. Mark wrote Mark, John wrote John. It's a fascinating book by someone who once believed what Sheila believes, and now, because of the evidence, has switched over to what I believe.

Mann: Sheila says that she is not biased. You apparently believe that she is. Do you have a question for her or a comment?

Morey: She has stated that she is an atheist and that she has joined an organization which is running around the country to do what they can to attack the Bible and Christianity. Obviously, that's a prejudiced person who has an axe to grind. So we are dealing with a prejudiced person like Madalyn Murray O'Hair.

Mann: Are you biased, Dr. Morey?

Morey: I approach the subject as a theist. She approaches it as an atheist. I want to go to the facts. She only wants to keep it to theory, not facts and—

Sheila: Oh, you're in trouble because the Bible says whatever is not faith is sin! You're in an awful lot of trouble if you're going to look for the facts. You're supposed to be basing everything on faith! Don't you know that as a theologian?

Mann: Dr. Morey, you're supposed to base everything on faith. Do you know that?

Morey: I do not think that the New Testament teaches that. She is reading one school of theologians such as Bultmann, who has a leap of faith which is an existential thing. That is not biblical or historic Christianity.

Sheila: I didn't get that from Bultmann. I got that straight out of the Bible. Now tell me why, if Paul was familiar with these Gospels, this so-called Lord's Prayer that has a God that's in control that says, "Oh, please don't lead us into temptation. God, please don't lead us into temptation"? Okay, when people say this Lord's Prayer, and the Gospels tell you how to pray, how's come Paul says we don't know how to pray?

Morey: Number one, she is taking several verses out of context. Number two, she is arguing from silence. When Paul said in Romans 8 that when we do not know what to say in our prayers, the Holy Spirit will help us, this refers to times when you're confused and don't know exactly what to say.

    The Lord's Prayer was not a liturgical prayer in the early part of the Christian Church. That's a modern phenomenon which I don't need to defend. My church doesn't repeat it, because it was not intended to be a liturgical prayer. So, she has taken verses out of context, mixed them together, rolled them out and come up with confusion.

Mann: All right, let's see if we can't get some listeners involved here. You're on the air.

Caller: The thought was brought up that Nazareth doesn't exist and wasn't mentioned in the Old Testament. I'd just like to say that I looked that up and the reason it wasn't mentioned in the Old Testament is that at the time of Christ it was only about 600 years old. If you know your Bible, you know that between Matthew and Malachi there is about a 400–year span. So Nazareth would not have existed into the writings of the prophets, the earlier writings in the Talmud, and the first five books of the Old Testament. So Nazareth existed at the time of Christ. It was about 600 years old and it exists today. You can go see it today. So that's not a valid thing for you to say.

Sheila: It didn't exist until the fourth century when people started going there as part of the Holy Lands.

Caller: It existed 600 years prior to Christ. Archaeology has proven that, madam.

One other thing: If you want to debate someone who knows something, then at least be polite to the person. Dr. Morey has done his homework. He doesn't do to you like you do to him. You're typical of most of these atheistic women libbers who like to castigate Paul because you say he hated women. Instead of saying something that you know from knowledge, you attack your opponent. You are very rude.

Sheila: I said that Paul hated women—and anyone who says it is good for a man not to touch a woman, and anyone who says the man is the head of the woman, and blames all the sins of the world onto the head of this woman who has eaten this piece of fruit from the tree is certainly not a man that I can respect.

Caller: We don't say that, madam. The Bible says what it says, and you're saying—

Sheila: I'm saying what Paul says. Paul is an historical writer and this is something that Paul said. This is one of the books that we do know that Paul wrote, right out of 1 and 2 Corinthians. Paul is a woman-hater. He is also someone who hated the pleasures of life. He was also someone who knew absolutely nothing about a Jesus of Nazareth.

Mann: Dr. Morey, do you look upon Paul as a woman-hater?

Morey: Well, once again she is taking verses out of context. If I had the time, Sheila, and if you ever get to central Pennsylvania, you are invited to my home. I've got over ten thousand volumes in my library. I would love to sit down with you because you haven't heard orthodox and historic theologians who—

Sheila: Okay, I'm going to ask you a direct question, and let's see if you can be honest enough to answer me directly on the radio. I want to know, do you believe that Jesus was divine or do you believe that there was a Jesus who was just a preacher, a flesh-and-blood preacher? And I want to know precisely what you believe.

Morey: I believe that Jesus Christ was God as well as man, that He was the incarnation of deity in human form.

Sheila: Okay, thanks for being honest. Now tell me what proof you have for that.

Morey: In the Old Testament it was predicted that the Messiah would be a God-man and the New Testament states that's exactly who Jesus was. He was given the names and the attributes of God, etc.

Sheila: Then, if this was a fact, the Jews would accept Jesus as the Messiah. But they do not accept Him!

Morey: Some Jews do. I go to the Messianic Conference where hundreds of Jewish Christians meet. It is twenty-five miles from my home. They meet every July.

Sheila: That's correct. Some do. But many of them don't, and they don't because it's not a fact.

There were many Christs, there were many Messiahs. This was an idea that was throughout history. There was Nestor, there was Krishna, there was Hercules, there were all of these savior myths that were similar things, with virgins being impregnated by gods. And can you imagine, of course, all these saviors ended up being male—the mothers many times being—

Mann: Okay, we're getting off on some subjects that would be fun to talk about another time. But, unfortunately, we don't have the time to get into all these things this afternoon. Let's give each of you thirty seconds to sum up your positions.

Sheila: There is absolutely no historical evidence for Jesus. This is not my opinion. This is the opinion of current biblical scholars—Protestant biblical scholars! They do not believe that there was a Jesus of Nazareth who said and did all of those wild things that we find Him saying and doing, like putting demons into pigs and they run into seas, and cursing fig trees and telling people they should eat His flesh.

Mann: Dr. Morey.

Morey: I would say there are many good Protestant theologians on my side, such as C. S. Lewis of Oxford, John Montgomery of Greenleaf Law School, F. F. Bruce of the University of Manchester, etc. I can name as many names as she can.

There is more historical evidence for Jesus Christ than for any other historical person. There are literary works from His friends and foes, archaeological evidence, letters, correspondence, and historians. Only the most biased atheist could possibly close their eyes to the dozens of historical evidences of the existence of Jesus.

Comments

The kind of arguments that Sheila used invariably involved logical fallacies. She argued from silence most of the time and she continually took statements out of context. One of her favorite methods was to commit the fallacy called "complex question," in which she made so many erroneous statements at one time that one had difficulty knowing where to begin. Most of her questions were based on wrong assumptions which should have been dealt with first.

If we took the skeptic's arguments and methodology which Sheila used to discredit the historical existence of Jesus Christ and applied them to any historical figure, the results would be disastrous. We would have to doubt the existence of all great men from Socrates to Abraham Lincoln. On the basis of the denial of the consequence, we must conclude that the methodology that the skeptic uses is erroneous and will result in absurd conclusions.

10

Jesus and Paul

The art of undercutting Christianity has always been a perilous business because the ongoing disciplines of archaeology and textual criticism have the nasty habit of crushing your pet theory under a pile of rude, ugly facts. The only safeguard is to maintain a fertile imagination and a dedication to endless speculation. Above all else, avoid any new scientific developments that would tend to discredit your theory.

How to Undercut a Religion

There are three basic ways to undercut a religion. The first is rather direct and calls for a daring spirit: *You simply deny that the founder ever existed!* This pulls the rug from under the religion. Once you've shown the founder to be totally legendary, the result of a busy imagination, you can dismiss the religion as mythical and therefore irrelevant.

To do this, you must never concern yourself with *proving* your denial. Just state it with great bravado and let the opposition run around trying to prove you wrong.

Desiring to discredit all religions in general, the rationalists of the nineteenth century advanced the notion that such religious figures as Abraham, Moses, Buddah, Jesus and Paul never existed. In the rationalists' opinion, such men were myths.

Thanks to the success of archaeology and related disciplines, however, no up-to-date scholar seriously questions that the founders of the major religions did, in fact, exist. All the archaeological evidence unearthed supports the historicity of these founders. Of course, there will be those who have not kept abreast of recent developments, and educationally still live in the nineteenth century. Now and then someone will claim Moses could not have written the Torah because there was no writing in his day!

When the evidence prevents you from denying the founder existed, a second method can be employed: *Drive a wedge between the founder and the religion which followed him.* If you can divorce the religion from the founder by demonstrating that the religion does not believe or practice as the founder did, you have effectively discredited the religion.

You should also claim that the religion obtained its beliefs and practices from some religious leader or leaders who came after the founder and corrupted his teachings. Boldly state that these corrupt leaders actually derived their concepts from religions which the founder would have viewed with hostility. Claim that one of these later leaders is the real founder of that religion.

Now you are ready for the third method: *You must categorically deny the reliability of the original writings of the religion,* insisting that these writings were tampered with by corrupt religious leaders. While doing this, ignore at all costs the science of textual criticism. Never attempt to *prove* that the text was corrupted. Just state that it was and continue your argument.

Sometimes it may help to state that these leaders destroyed the "true" original documents of the religion. Let your imagination go wild at this point. State that these missing documents taught all sorts of beliefs which conflict with the religion supposedly derived from them. Since you claim that all the evidence was destroyed, no one can disprove you. Of course, never accept the burden of proof that these missing documents actually existed.

This third method proves particularly useful if you are faced with a statement in the existing original documents which contradicts your theory. The important thing to remember is to argue in a circle.

Whenever the documents state something you can use, claim such statements to be reliable and authentic. But whenever you run across statements in the documents which contradict your position, always claim such statements to be corruptions, interpolations, etc. In this way, you can always dismiss with ease anything which may refute your position. Of course, never attempt to *prove* these annoying statements are corruptions. Just state they are and proceed.

The following illustration of how these methods have been applied to both Judaism and Christianity may prove helpful.

JUDAISM	CHRISTIANITY
1. Abraham, Moses, David, etc. never existed. They are myths.	1. Jesus, Paul and the Apostles never existed.
2. Moses is not the founder of Judaism. The Torah is the work of subsequent leaders and does not reflect the beliefs or practices of Moses. The origin of Judaism is to be found in the ancient pagan religions. The Writings and the Prophets did not interpret the Law of Moses. They corrupted it.	2. Jesus is not the founder of Christianity. The Gospels are the work of subsequent leaders and do not reflect the beliefs or practices of Jesus. Paul and the Apostles developed Christianity from the religions around them. The New Testament epistles did not interpret the teaching of Jesus. They corrupted it.
3. The Jewish Bible is historically unreliable. It is composed of groundless myths.	3. The Christian Bible is historically unreliable. It is composed of groundless myths.

A Case in Point

In the August 1984 issue of *Commentary*, Hyam Maccoby resurrects a theology originally developed by Wrede in 1904. In *Paulus*, Wrede states that Paul was the true founder of

Christianity and that Paul's religion was not the religion of Jesus. This was further developed by Bruckner in 1908. In his *Der Sterbe und Auferstehende Gottheiland,* he claimed that Paul derived Christianity from the Greek mystery cults. This was repeated again by Bousset in his *Kyrious Christos* in 1913. It was fully answered by the great Princeton scholar Gresham Machen in his *Origin of Paul's Religion* in 1925. The Dutch scholar H. Ridderbos brought the debate up-to-date once again in 1958 in his *Paul and Jesus.* The facts are as follows:

1. The historicity of Jesus and His Apostles cannot be validly denied. Archaeologists frequently unearth more evidence to verify this.

2. A wedge cannot arbitrarily be driven between Paul and Jesus.

3. Christianity is the religion founded by Jesus and expounded by the Apostles (Paul included). Opponents often forget the New Testament is composed of books written by Apostles such as Peter and John, as well as Paul. There is no evidence that the Apostles who had lived with Jesus accused Paul of contradicting Jesus.

4. Christianity cannot be reduced to Jewish Apocalypticism. The attempt to identify the New Testament concept of the person and work of Jesus with various intertestamental movements or literature has borne no fruit. Jesus does not fit the apocalyptic picture of the Messiah who was expected to come.

5. Christianity cannot be relegated to the Greek mystery religions. No evidence exists that the mystery religions which preceded the appearance of Christianity had any "Christian" concepts. None of these Greek religions had the concept of a substitutionary atonement and bodily resurrection found in the New Testament. Further research since 1908 has demonstrated that the attempt to identify the annual fall and spring festivals of pagan fertility gods such as Osiris, Attis, etc., with the New Testament concept of the death and resurrection of Jesus can no longer be viewed as valid. After all, one can stretch the imagination only so far!

Hyam Maccoby, and the writers on which he depends,

merely repeat the old arguments from 1908. They do not give any evidence of having read Machen's classic work on the subject or knowing any of the major contemporary works on Paul which stand against their theory (see F. F. Bruce, Ridderbos, etc.). They simply utilize the methodology outlined in the first section of this chapter. They treat the New Testament as if the reliability of statements in the Gospels depends entirely on whether or not the statements fit their preconceived notions.

In the light of what we know, we must conclude that no one has clearly established one simple historical source for Christianity. Instead, we should consider the following information:

1. Some of the concepts found in the New Testament are unique and cannot be reduced to anything in the Hebrew or Hellenistic world.

2. Any investigation into the origin of Christianity must examine the passages from the Law and Prophets which Jesus and the Apostles interpreted in the New Testament. After all, the Apostles claimed that Jesus was the Messiah because He fulfilled the messianic prophecies in the Old Testament.

3. Jesus and the Apostles never appealed to apocalyptic works. There is no evidence that they depended on any one form of contemporary Judaism. The claim that they were Essenes or members of some cultic movement has no basis in fact.

4. We must not neglect the existential impact of the visions which the Apostles claimed to receive from God. These visions revealed new concepts. Why should we arbitrarily assume that these revelations were ideas borrowed from contemporary Judaism or paganism? Why couldn't they be new? Peter's vision concerning the Gentiles (Acts 10) or the revelations which Paul claimed to receive from the heavenly Jesus (Gal. 1) and the other visions recorded in the New Testament should no longer be ignored.

5. Just as modern Jewish scholars have finally reclaimed Jesus' validity and have dropped the polemics of the past, there is a growing movement to reclaim the validity of the Apostle Paul.

The arguments once given against Jesus, and now admitted to be biased and false, were arbitrarily transferred to Paul. If the same accusations were invalid when applied to Jesus, they should be equally invalid when applied to Paul or to one of the other apostles.

Conclusion

There exist no solid reasons for viewing Paul as the sole founder of Christianity. The attempt to do so has generally come from hostile, biased individuals who wish to undercut Christianity. They cannot be viewed as impartial researchers, but as people with an ax to grind.

The methodology described in this chapter is that used by some people in their attempt to undercut Christianity. We should realize that this approach to religion in general, and Christianity in particular, has never produced positive results because it is filled with logical and methodological blunders of titanic proportions. New archaeological discoveries have tumbled dozens of such speculative systems.

These opponents of Christianity never discuss why they *assume* Jesus was not who He claimed to be. They never demonstrate why they *assume* the Bible is unreliable. Such unwarranted assumptions are unworthy of an enlightened mind willing to seek the Truth wherever it can be found.

11

Atheists in Action

We can learn about something by observing it in action. Seeing how it functions, and what it accomplishes or produces can be an education in itself. While such a procedure is usually connected only with mechanical devices, it can be applied with great profit to intellectual matters where opposing sides debate the issues. This approach was used with great profit by Socrates in his *Dialogues* and by Christ in the Gospels.

During the last twenty years I have debated and dialogued with many atheists. Some of my experiences may prove quite helpful in understanding how an atheist will argue his case. After all, the ins and outs of a philosophical position can at times be more clear in the heat of debate than when confined to the pages of a book, because there is no room for building a straw man when the real opponent is present in the flesh.

In the following cases, observe the structure and methodology the atheist uses in his arguments. Notice the way he deals with the issues. Pay attention to any assumptions he makes.

Observe also, with equal scrutiny, the way the theist approaches the issues and handles the arguments. But, since the main focus of this book is on atheism and not on theism, focus on the atheist and how he argues his case.

Case #1

Christian students at the Juilliard School of Music in New York City were being hassled by an atheistic professor who used class time to attack belief in God and Christianity. Since he taught musicology and not philosophy, his constant attempts to convert students to atheism had progressed to the point where he was mocking the Christian students and using ridicule to score points against theism.

Feeling they had tolerated enough, the students asked him if he would like to debate the issues with a theist at one of their meetings. He agreed to debate the atheist position and even arranged for a classroom to be used. Because the students and I attended the same church in New York City, and because I had attended several of their meetings at Juilliard, they asked me to debate the atheistic professor. The Christians publicized the coming debate and arranged for as many students to come as possible.

The atheist was given the opportunity to begin the debate. His opening statement was:

> I am so happy to have all of you together at last. You see, the Bible says that "when I was a child, I thought and acted like a child. But now that I am an adult, it is time to put away childish things." This is what I have been trying to tell you students.
>
> You and I used to believe in Santa Claus when we were children. But we no longer believe in him, do we? It is the same way with God. God is for childish minds. No adult should believe in Him any more than believing in Santa Claus. You see, there is no God. He does not exist any more than Santa. I know the Bible says "the fool says there is no God," but I say that only a fool believes in God.
>
> This is all I really have to say. Atheism is simply a matter of giving up childish beliefs.

He sat down at this point and I was asked to give the theist's opening statement.

> I appreciate the frankness of Professor ———. It isn't every day that the cards are laid on the table so quickly in a debate. The thesis that he gave us was quite simple and clear. He said, "There is no God."

In order for me to make my presentation, I need the assistance of the professor. Would you please join me once again at the front of the classroom?

He agreed and came forward.

Would you please take this piece of chalk and come to the blackboard with me? Thank you.

We now stood at the blackboard. For the dialogue which follows, *A* will denote what the atheist said and *T* what the theist said.

T: Now, would you make a dot on the blackboard. It does not have to be big. For the purposes of this illustration, this dot represents you. Is this all right with you?

A: Oh, I don't see why not.

T: Would you now draw a circle around that dot with the dot in the center of the circle. The inside of the circle represents what you know; what you studied or experienced; where you have been; what you have seen and heard. The outside of the circle represents what you do not know; what you haven't studied or experienced; where you have not gone or seen or heard.

Now, obviously in this age of specialization, there will be more outside the circle than what is in the circle. Since your degree is in musicology, would you claim to know a great deal about—let's say, nuclear physics or quantum mechanics?

A: No, I admit that I am limited in knowledge.

T: Given that this is the case, how much is outside of the circle in comparison with what is inside it?

A: Well, I can't guess that.

T: What I mean is that if you walked through the Library of Congress, how many of the subjects would you say you knew?

A: Well, I guess I would have to admit that I would know only a fraction of the knowledge that is out there.

T: You would agree that it would be in the decimal points. We would all have to say that our knowledge would be something like .0000001%. But for the purposes of this illustration, we will say that you have one percent of all knowledge. Would you please write 1% in the inside of the circle? Thank you.

Now, how much is outside the circle?

A: I guess that it would be 99%.

T: Please write 99% outside the circle. Thank you. Now, would you please hand me the chalk? Now, remember that what is outside of the circle is what you admit you do not know.

(I drew an X outside the circle.) Is it possible for God to exist outside the circle of your experience and knowledge? Is it logically possible for God to exist outside the circle? What if "God" lived in Argentina? Have you been to Argentina?

A: I would have to admit that I have never been to Argentina. But I don't think that this is fair.

T: You see, the point of my opening statement is that it is philosophically and logically absurd to state such a universal negative as, "There is no God." The only one who can say that there are no gods of any size, shape, or form in the universe throughout all of time is God himself! You would have to have been all places at the same time with perfect knowledge of all of time to know that God does not exist. In short, you have to be omnipresent and omniscient to have such knowledge. And in order to pull off the whole thing, you would have to be omnipotent as well!

Now, I asked you, is it possible for God to exist outside the circle of your limited knowledge and experience?

A: Well, I would have to admit that God could exist outside the circle. But I think that it is impossible to know if He does. This debate is not fair. I did not know that I would have to deal with this man.

T: You said, if I heard you correctly, that it is logically impossible to say that God does not exist?

A: Yes, I admit it. You see, I am really not an atheist. I am an agnostic. I don't know if God exists.

T: Well, then I have won the debate. You have presented yourself to these students as an atheist all year long and now you have admitted in front of them that atheism is not logically possible. You agreed that it is a false theory. Instead, you now claim to be an agnostic.

A: I didn't know that this is what I was going to get into when I agreed to come to your meeting. I don't think this is fair at all.

T: Since we have refuted atheism together, perhaps you would be willing to discuss agnosticism? That would be a totally new debate. Would you be willing to discuss agnosticism?

A: I don't know if I care to discuss the issue with you.

T: At least tell us what kind of agnostic you are.

A: What kind?

T: Yes. There are two basic kinds: The ordinary agnostic says, "I don't know if God exists, but if you can show me from the circle of my own knowledge and experience that God exists, I will believe in Him."

This is in opposition to the ornery agnostic who dogmatically states, "*I* don't know if God exists and *you* don't know if God exists because *no one* can ever know if He does or doesn't. It is impossible to know if God exists."

A: Well, I hope that I am an ordinary agnostic.

T: Then you are willing to look inside the circle of your knowledge and experience to see if there are any evidences of God's existence? This means that you will not make any leaps of faith to abstract ideas that we cannot experience.

A: What do you mean?

T: For example, if we begin to discuss the relationship between cause and effect, you won't up and say that there are "causeless effects" or that you do not believe in "cause and effect." After all, *you* have never experienced something which was without a cause, have you? If you hear a noise in your house in the middle of the night, you get up and investigate its cause. You don't roll over and go back to sleep saying that the noise does not have a cause.

Or, if I appeal to the principle that something has to get the ball rolling, you will not say that motion can be eternal and without a cause, for you have never experienced a causeless and eternal motion. If you walk into a room and see a pool ball rolling across the table, you would never in your right mind say that the ball either started rolling all by itself or has been rolling around on that table for all eternity.

Or again, if I appeal to the Second Law of Thermodynamics, in which the universe is running down, you will not say that the universe has been running down for all eternity and need not have a beginning. Have you ever had a clock that ran down that had *not* been first wound up?

In other words, we will limit ourselves to what you have really experienced and leave off abstract ideas that simply don't conform to life as it is.

A: I don't care to continue the debate any further. It is over so far as I am concerned.

T: Then in terms of your original position of atheism, you admit defeat?

A: I don't admit anything. (He walked out of the room at this point.)

T: I hope the audience enjoyed my debate with Professor—. In terms of his original thesis, he had to admit that he was logically and philosophically absurd to say that there is no God. I was willing to go on and debate agnosticism and the theistic proofs. But, seeing that he has left the room in a hurry, perhaps you can persuade him that a second debate is necessary.

The professor later refused my offer but at least he stopped hassling the students for the rest of the semester.

Case #2

On one of my radio shows I debated an atheist who had recently written a book against God. The debate bogged down at the very beginning when we could not agree on the definition of atheism. He argued that an atheist states nothing and believes nothing. Thus he does not have to prove anything. He does not say that there is no God. Atheism is simply the absence of belief in God.

My objections to this fideistic definition have already been given in the chapter on defining atheism. The debate continued when he asked me what my position was.

T: My position is that atheism is false for several reasons: It is philosophically absurd, scientifically erroneous, morally bankrupt, socially destructive, aesthetically impotent, and humanly degrading. I intend to put you on the hot seat for a change. Instead of the theist being on the defensive, the atheist is going to have to defend the validity of what he believes.

A: But, I do not want to defend atheism. I want you to defend theism. Let's discuss the theistic proofs.

T: But, if you remember, when we contacted you, we stated that the discussion would be on atheism and your book.

A: Well, I guess so. So, go on with your presentation.

T: I say atheism is philosphically absurd because it is impossible to prove a universal negative. You must agree with me because you made up your fideistic definition of atheism in order to avoid the very error I am referring to. I say it is scientifically erroneous because atheists believe that the universe is eternal, self-sustaining and causeless.

A: But atheists have no beliefs.

T: Do you *believe* that the universe exists or is it an illusion or dream?

A: I don't *believe* it exists; it simply exists.

T: But to *say* it exists is to tell me what you believe. I have met those who say that it doesn't exist. So, I ask you, is this universe without a beginning? Is it eternal or not? What do you believe?

A: But, as I told you, I don't have any beliefs. So why are you asking me about my beliefs?

T: You cannot legitimately pretend to be without beliefs because you wrote your book. In it you state that you *believe* in a lot of things. You said that you believed in rationalism. You claimed to believe in science, didn't you? In other words, you believe in a lot of things such as materialism and rationalism. You can't fool everybody! You believe in a godless universe. And since it is godless, it is also eternal, self-sustaining and self-renewing.

These beliefs do not square with the scientific facts that the universe had a beginning and is now running down.

You also appeal to chance an awful lot in your book. Chance is your "god" who does all things magically. Whenever you can't answer a question, you say, "It happened by chance."

I also say that atheism is morally bankrupt because as Sartre and Nietzsche have demonstrated, without God as the universal reference point to distinguish good from evil, there are no absolute morals. Man becomes the measure of all things, including his own ethics and morality.

I know your argument that God cannot be the standard of goodness because of the statement "God is good." But it doesn't hold any water for two reasons: First, the normal meaning of the statement is that God has done things which the believer feels are good to him, i.e., "God is good to me." This is its subjective and personal meaning.

Secondly, when a Christian says "God is good" as a description of the character of God, he is saying that the God of the Bible fits the description of the true God who is the ultimate Good. He is saying that his God in opposition to, let's say, the Muslim's god, is the true one, i.e., the Christian God fits the bill of the true God.

To say that the true God who is the ultimate Good does not exist because a Christian identifies his God as this ultimate Good is not logical. Let me put it another way. To say that X does not exist because someone claims that Y has the properties of X is illogical.

Atheism is clearly socially destructive because it always leads to tyranny. Either the state or God is ultimate. Thus atheists look to the state to function in the place of God. The state decides the purpose and meaning of man. The state should provide for all things. The state is the ultimate reference point for truth as well as morals. Thus it always ends in the destruction of freedom. Just look at what atheism has done to Russia or Cuba. Over one hundred and fifty million people in the last forty years have been killed by atheistic governments.

Atheism is also an economic disaster—as history shows. When a country is taken over by an atheistic government, they can't even feed themselves. The economy is ruined and they must depend on the West for their daily bread.

I also say that atheism is aesthetically impotent. If we look to see what religion has produced in terms of art, there is no question but that faith in God has inspired man to the highest expressions of art possible. Be it paintings, sculpture, music, literature or architecture, faith in God has given the world its greatest treasures. But what has atheism given the world? Ugliness is the only thing. The ugliness of John Cage's music or modern art. Its themes are discord, confusion and despair. There is nothing in atheism that gives hope and light to the human soul. It is a philosophy of despair.

And I say that it is humanly degrading because it reduces man to an animal or a machine. As Skinner demonstrated, without God, man has no dignity or freedom. People can be treated like an animal if this is all you think they are. The stench of Hitler's ovens is the perfume that adorns atheism.

A: I really don't think that it is of any use to go any further. I am not going to defend atheism. I will discuss theism and why people believe in God. But I refuse to discuss atheism or try to defend it.

We went a few more rounds, but he did not want to answer my charges concerning atheism.

Case #3

I probably will never forget my long nights as a counselor at The Catacombs, a Christian coffee house in Greenwich Village of New York City. Because the place was packed every night until 2:00 or 3:00 a.m., I often didn't arrive home until 4:00 a.m. (There is a certain charm about the "naked city" that one cannot witness unless he travels the city late at night.)

With the crazy sixties in full swing, the anti-Vietnam War hysteria was at its height and drugs were increasing in popularity. Not surprisingly, The Catacombs was swamped with young atheists, who nightly provided endless discussions about religion, politics and drugs. Greenwich Village was where "the action was," and The Catacombs was a great success.

Hundreds of people came to The Catacombs for the free coffee and donuts, or because the establishment was warm in the winter and cool in the summer, but a dedicated group of atheists and homosexuals came regularly to butt heads with the Christians. It was a first-class training ground for young theists and atheists. I could not have asked for a better situation.

One night, at about 2:00 a.m., a young Jewish girl named Susan entered The Catacombs with her newest boyfriend. As the night had been a slow one for her, she had come to do some "bear baiting." She ended up at my table because the other counselors had the nasty habit of sending over all the "tough" cases for me to handle.

Susan had shown up several times, always with a different boy in tow. This night she was in a nasty mood. Maybe it was some drug she was on. We will pick up the conversation at this point.

T: I am glad to see you again, Susan.

A: Well, I see they stuck me with you again.

T: It can't be all that bad. Shall I get you some coffee and donuts?

A: Yea, you might as well.

T: Have you thought about our last conversation?

A: Yes. Even though I haven't thought of a way around it yet, I'll keep trying. You haven't won yet.

T: But you must agree that we have made some progress. Remember the axiom of existence, the principle of motion, the reality of order, the need for a moral absolute and all the other things we looked at?

A: Yea, I remember. But I still don't believe in God. The question I came to ask you tonight is, why do you believe in the Bible? I mean you *really* believe in it, don't you? I want a straightforward answer. How do you know it is true?

T: Why, *you* have proved the Bible to me. Every word you have said was exactly what the Bible predicted you would say.

A: What do you mean that *I* have proved the Bible! I don't want to prove the Bible.

T: Well, do you feel that the gospel which I have shared with you is foolishness?

A: Of course it is!

T: Then you just proved 1 Corinthians 1:18 which says that the gospel is foolishness to those who are lost. Do you fear God at all, Susan?

A: No.

T: Then you just proved Romans 3:18, which predicted that you would not fear God.

A: But I don't want to prove the Bible!

T: But every word you speak and everything you do is a confirmation of the Bible. Do you believe in the Ten Commandments? If you don't, and I know that you don't, then the Bible predicts that you will probably engage in immorality. Your immorality and drug use prove the Bible.

A: But I don't see how my sex life proves the Bible.

T: Well, you asked me how I know that the Bible is true. One of the reasons I believe in the Bible is that everything in life that I see and experience conforms exactly with what the Bible says I will see and experience. And you have made me a stronger believer every time you have opened your mouth. And I thank you for proving the Bible to me.

Her boyfriend came over at this point and said that they had to get going. I was to leave New York City that week to return to college, and the thought that I would probably never see her again saddened me.

Case #4

During my years in graduate school I took a summer job with General Motors in a plant near Chicago. One man at the plant was an aggressive atheist who often tried to start an argument with any believers at work. John seemed to take special delight in playing the devil's advocate with me and was always coming up with some new argument against theism. He was quite confident that he had all the answers. On one occasion he asked me:

A: Morey, I've been thinking about something that you can't answer. I'm referring to the problem of evil. If your God is good, why hasn't He solved the problem of evil?

   Because He doesn't want to? Then He isn't good.

   But if the problem is that He *can't* solve the problem of evil, then He is not all-powerful. So, take your pick. Either God is not good or He is not all-powerful. And don't try to squirm out of this with that free-will crap you theists are always throwing around.

T: Well, John, I have a question for you before we begin. How many books have you read on the problem of evil? If you are really concerned about evil, I want to know if you have ever studied the issue. So, how many books have you read on the subject?

A: I haven't read any books on it. But what does that matter?

T: Well, it matters a great deal. If you are only throwing up a challenge to me instead of asking an honest question, it matters a great deal to me.

A: But I do want to hear your answer, honestly.

T: Let's talk about it at lunch time, for I have a few friends who would like to get in on this discussion.

   (Later at lunch break, the discussion picked up again.)

T: You have asked me about the problem of evil. And you have said that you have already ruled out the idea of free will, right?

A: That's right. I don't want to hear about free will.

T: I don't think that it is logically valid for you to assume that free will does not enter into the problem before you even hear where it enters into my answer. I will bring it up at one point, if for no other reason than for you to understand how I as a Christian answer your challenge. Okay?

A: All right.

T: There are two points I wish to make at the outset. First, answer this question: Do you believe in moral absolutes or do you believe that everything is relative?

A: There are no absolutes. Everything is relative. I know it and you know it.

T: Then the first thing you must do is to prove the existence of evil. After all, there are Eastern philosophies which deny the existence of evil. As the Christian Scientists, they answer the problem of evil by denying there is any evil to have a problem with.

A: Of course evil exists. Look around you—it's everywhere.

T: But *how* do you know evil when you see it? By what process do you identify evil? Assuming that evil exists, and assuming you can identify it are two different things.

My point is that, as Socrates demonstrated a long time ago, to make a distinction between particulars in which one is good and one is evil, you must have a universal or absolute to do it. Once you see this, then the ultimate result is that without an infinite reference point for "good," no one can identify what is good or evil. God alone can exhaust the meaning of an infinite good. Thus without the existence of God, there is no "evil" or "good" in an absolute sense but everything is relative. The problem of evil does not negate the existence of God. It actually requires it. I just want to make this clear from the outset.

A: What you are trying to say is that there is no evil if there is no God? But I believe that evil exists, but I don't believe that God exists. This fact refutes your position.

T: Maybe I was not clear on something. When I say the word "evil," I am talking in an absolute way and not in a relative sense. You are using the word evil in a relative sense. Remember that you do not believe in absolutes. Everything is relative according to you.

For example, I would say that adultery is evil regardless of who, what, when or how. It is absolutely wrong regardless of the situation. When I say it is evil, it is absolutely evil. Is this what you believe?

A: No. There are situations where adultery is probably the right thing to do. You see, I don't believe that anything is evil in an absolute way.

T: That is my point. You don't really believe in evil in the sense as I believe in it because you don't believe in God. You are committing a basic error in logic in which you are giving a different definition to the word "evil" than what I meant by it. When I said that you can't believe in evil if you don't believe in God, I was right, because you don't believe in absolute evil and good. That you claim to believe in evil in a relative sense has nothing logically to do with my argument.

A: So, we both believe in evil in our own way. How does this answer the problem of evil?

T: This brings up the second point which is this: Why do you assume that God has not already solved the problem of evil in such a way that neither His goodness nor omnipotence is limited? On what grounds do you limit what God can or cannot do to solve this problem?

A: You don't believe that God has solved the problem of evil, do you? I have never met a theist who did.

T: Well, you've met one now. You see, I believe that God has already solved the problem of evil. And He did it in a way in which He did not contradict His nature or the nature of man.

A: You're going to sit there and tell me that evil no longer exists? That evil is now gone? That's insane! Evil is still present in this world.

T: This is why I warned you about limiting God in terms of how He solves the problem. You assume that God can solve the problem only in one single act. But why can't He deal with evil in a progressive way? Why does He have to deal with it all at once? Can't He deal with it throughout time as we know it and then bring it to climax on the Day of Judgment? You are assuming that the only way for God to deal with evil is in one single act. This is an erroneous assumption on your part. I am not saying that evil no longer exists. I am saying that God has solved the problem but in a long-term way, in stages.

A: When did God solve the problem of evil? I don't see it.

T: God sent His Son to die on the cross in order to solve the problem of evil. Christ atoned for evil and secured the eventual removal of all evil from the earth. One day evil will be quarantined in one spot called hell. Then there will be a perfect world devoid of all evil.

A: I can't say that I like this solution to evil. I have never heard this approach before. It seems to me that evil should be just done away with, or something. Why must God take all of history to get the job done?

T: Let's take the suggestion you made. If God declared that all evil would, at this moment, cease to exist, you and I and all of humanity would go up in a puff of smoke. Does this seem to be a good solution to you?

A: Well, I didn't mean that. But can't He just make everyone good or stop people from doing evil?

T: But this would mean the destruction of man as *man*. Would man be man if he no longer could choose? Aren't you saying that all men should become robots? This still means that man, as we know him, would be destroyed.

Besides violating man's nature, if God did not punish evil, He would deny His nature as well. Divine justice demands that sin be punished. Christ took the punishment that justice demands—on behalf of His people. Those who reject Christ must pay the price that justice demands. They pay for their evil in this life and in the life to come.

A: But I don't believe that Jesus ever solved the problem of evil. There has to be a better way to solve evil than what you are saying.

T: Well, let's put it to the test. I will give you the next five minutes to come up with a solution that does not destroy man or make God deny His own nature. Go. . . .
(He sat and concentrated for the full five minutes.)

A: I must admit that I'm stumped. I can't think of another way—but that does not mean that your solution is right. I'll have to think about this one. When I come up with something, I'll let you know.

T: I know that five minutes isn't enough. Take all the time you need.

Before returning to school at the end of the summer, I made a point of seeking John out. I asked him, "John, did you solve the problem of evil?"

He replied, "No. I have no answer."

I took him by the shoulders and looked him in the eyes and said, "John, you know that there is a God and that one day you are going to stand before Him."

Tears came to his eyes as he said, "Yes, I know it. But I don't know what to do about it."

"John," I responded, "either you are part of the problem of evil or you are part of its solution. Jesus Christ is your only hope. Seek Him while He may be found, for He is not far from all who call upon Him." He promised to read the Bible and to seek salvation. I look forward to seeing him in heaven one day.

Case #5

This case involves a Jewish woman in Central Park. After church one Sunday, several of us went to Central Park to have a picnic and to listen to some sermons on our tape recorder. While we were listening to the sermon, a man and a woman quietly joined our group and listened until the sermon was over. Then before any of us had the opportunity to speak, the woman jumped up and screamed at us as she pulled up her sleeve and showed us a number tatooed on her arm.

"There is no God, I tell you. If there is a God, why did He let Hitler kill six million Jews? You see this number? I was in one of Hitler's concentration camps. All my family died there except for me. I tell you, there is no God. How can you believe in a God who would allow Hitler to do what he did?"

She went on for several minutes and we were at first too stunned to respond. It would have been impossible to get a word in edgewise until she had spewed out all her hatred and bitterness. When she seemed to have calmed down, I said:

T: Madam! Madam! I have only one question to ask you: If there is no God, then on what grounds do you judge Hitler? How do you know that he was evil? How do you know that what he did was wrong?

A: Of course he was evil!

T: But how do you know that he was? Without God there is no Day of Judgment when people like Hitler will be punished for the evil they do. Without the Day of Judgment, there is no ultimate justice in this world. Hitler will go scot-free. Do you really believe that there is no day of reckoning for evil? Madam, you need God in order to condemn Hitler. If there is no God, then there are no moral absolutes by which you have the right to judge someone else.

A: But I don't believe in judging anyone.

T: Then how do you judge Hitler? He felt he was doing a good thing for his people. He wanted to purify the race, to rebuild the country, and the Jews—in his mind—were in the way of his goals.

A: Are you saying that Hitler was right when he killed all those people?

T: No. But because I do believe in God, I know that Hitler was an evil man. He broke God's law when he murdered untold millions. But if I don't believe in God, I have no right to say that he was right or wrong.

A: I never thought about it this way.

T: I am sure you haven't. But be assured by us that Hitler did not escape justice. There is a Day of Judgment and he will not escape the judgment of God in hell. But what about you? You too will stand before God one day. Without Yeshua to save you, how will you ever say, *"Shema Yisrael! Adonai Eloheynu, Adonai Echad."* Look to Yeshua, for He is King Messiah.

She took a New Testament and some literature we offered her, and she promised to study them.

Case #6

One last case will illustrate some of the logical implications of atheism. This scene took place one afternoon in the living room of a young infidel who was deeply involved in the civil rights struggles of the sixties.

T: I think you have a real problem living what you believe. I mean, you have to live as if you are a theist. How else could you be involved in civil rights?

A: I fail to see any relationship between religion and civil rights.

T: Let me explain. Do you believe in the Bible?

A: No.

T: Then you don't believe that God made Adam and Eve?

A: No. I believe in evolution.

T: Exactly what I hoped you would say! Where did the different races come from? From different ancestral primates? Thus the races evolved from different origins?

A: That's what many scientists believe.

T: Where did the concept of "mankind" come from? Why do we speak of "man" or "humanity"? Historically, we got the concept from the biblical idea that all people descended from Adam and Eve. Thus the unity of mankind depends on whether you accept the biblical concept.

Also, where do you get the idea that human beings have dignity? You fight for the blacks to get the dignity they deserve. But what if no one deserves any dignity? If the blacks are just one species of primates which spun out of a different origin than the white race, and the blacks as well as the whites are only animals, why shouldn't they treat each other as animals? What's wrong with southern whites using cattle prods on black animals if that is all they really are?

Since you assume evolution to be true, doesn't your civil rights work stand in the way of the survival of the fittest? If the whites are stronger, shouldn't they make the blacks slaves? The unity and dignity of humanity depends entirely on the religious base found in the Bible.

A: I really don't care what you say. I don't believe in God but I do believe in civil rights. And nothing you will ever say can change that.

Summary

The above cases serve well in showing how an atheist will defend his beliefs as well as his unbelief. Such issues as civil rights, the dignity of man, and the moral condemnation of evil, require the existence of God. The atheist, in taking a moral stand on these issues, must therefore live on the borrowed capital he derives from the Judeo-Christian base of Western society.

As Christianity is replaced by secularism, we will see the end of the unity and dignity of man. The abortion clinics will pave the way for euthanasia centers. "Mercy" killing will lead to the genocide of entire racial, social and religious groups. Hitler's and Lenin's dreams will yet find their fulfillment in a secular world which acknowledges no moral guidelines because it acknowledges no God.

Conclusion

We have examined modern atheism in terms of its history, motives, political expression, internal structure, and the methodologies by which it argues. Atheism attempts to do that which is impossible—as man will never cease to be religious because that is part of his humanness. Attempts to deny this aspect of man have resulted in the greatest inhumanities the world has ever seen.

The genocide of the peaceful Cambodians, the planned starving of Ethiopians, and the wholesale slaughter of Central American Indians are only three present examples of the forces unleashed by modern unbelief and its crusade against God. In its rejection of God, it has rejected man. In its fight against God, it is fighting against everything noble in man.

May this study of atheism effectively inform and alert people to the arguments and tactics they will increasingly face as the forces of secularism continue their downward path toward Orwell's tyrannical brave new world.

For the theist who yields to the claims of Jesus Christ, however, there is a new world coming. A world delivered from all evil through the atoning work of the Son of God, King Messiah. To Him be all the glory!

Appendix

Answers to Common Objections

In the following chart, many of the common objections to religion are traced to the real problem, the hidden presupposition which is the root issue. Then a theistic answer is given. The chart is not to be viewed as something to memorize but rather as illustrations of how to trace surface objections to the hidden presuppositions. Instead of spending fruitless time dealing with surface objections, we must uncover the hidden assumptions which produced the objection in the first place.

SURFACE OBJECTIONS	PRESUPPOSITIONS	CHRISTIAN ANSWERS
Jesus was a good man and a great teacher . . . that is all He was.	Jesus was a great human being. No one can deny this . . . *but He was not God* or the Christ.	This statement is self-refuting. If Jesus was a good man and a great teacher, then we must accept what He taught about himself—that is, that He is God the Son, the Savior of the world. If He is not who He claimed to be, He was either a liar or a lunatic. If He was a liar or a lunatic, He was not a good man *or a great teacher!*
Man is not evil, but good.	People are basically good. It is their environment that makes them bad. Give them good education, housing, and jobs, and people will be good.	This statement does not correspond to reality. History and psychology give irrefutable proof that man is corrupt in his very nature. No one need teach children to lie, steal, cheat, etc. Hitler's Germany was the most highly educated country in the world. The Scriptures are verified by *all* data when it says, "The heart is deceitful . . . and desperately wicked" (Jer. 17:9 KJV).
Christianity is a psychological crutch.	People accept Christianity because it meets some psychological need in them. Thus, it cannot be the true religion.	Christianity is shown to be true because it *does* meet all the needs of man, including his psychological needs. Since God created man, He knows what man needs. Thus, it is only logical to assume that the religion which God reveals will meet those needs. This position actually proves what it set out to refute.
I'm an atheist. I do not believe in God.	They assume that they are competent to come to this position. They feel that there is no deity of any shape, size, or form.	The only person who can be an atheist is God himself. To say dogmatically, "There is no God!" requires one to know all things, to be all places at the same time, and have all power. Thus, you would have to be omniscient, omnipresent, and omnipotent, i.e., God! Atheism is a theological absurdity. It is self-refuting.

SURFACE OBJECTIONS	PRESUPPOSITIONS	CHRISTIAN ANSWERS
If Christianity works for you and makes you feel good, fine . . . but don't bug *me* with it!	Everyone should do his "thing." As long as he doesn't bother others, it's okay. Truth and morality are not important. Only the individual pursuit of pleasure is right!	This is crude selfishness. The Christian's task *is* to "bug" others! Hedonistic lifestyles have always led to disaster. Just because something "feels good" does not make it right. Psychotic killers "feel good" as they murder their victims! This position is unlivable.
I am not a sinner.	A "sinner" is a social outcast—a whore, a drunkard, etc. This person is self-righteous, upright, and morally respectable.	All people are sinners, though in various degrees. A "sinner" is one who has not done all he should, and who has done what he should not have done. Sin is true guilt before God. God demands 100% of us keeping 100% of the law, 100% of the time. Anything less is sin.
I'm too evil for Christianity. God would never accept me.	Christianity is for good, respectable people, not for "sinners." God can never forgive really *bad* people.	According to the Bible, "good people" go to hell, and "bad" people go to heaven! Jesus said that He did not come to call *righteous* people, but *sinners*. Christianity holds out hope only for those who sense their unworthiness and sinfulness. To such, Christ says, "Come unto me!"
I don't believe that Jesus rose from the dead.	The universe is a closed system, controlled by the laws of nature, which are absolute and unbreakable. Since the resurrection of Christ was a miracle, it is *impossible*, since miracles *cannot* happen.	The universe is not "run" or "held together" by any so-called "laws." God is personally upholding and running the universe (Col. 1:17; Eph. 1:11). Miracles do not violate "laws," because "laws" are simply human observations of the ways God upholds the universe. Modern science now rejects the Newtonian mechanistic world and life view which lies behind the objection.

163

SURFACE OBJECTIONS	PRESUPPOSITIONS	CHRISTIAN ANSWERS
I don't accept the Bible.	Human autonomy: man starting *from* himself, *by* himself, *without* any outside special revelation, *can* understand himself and the world around him with all the interrelationships involved. This has always been the vain hope of the humanist.	The history of philosophy shows that human autonomy ends in total skepticism. If we start with man, we end in total confusion. Only as we start with God is the universe intelligible. The surface objection does not correspond with reality. (See Francis Schaeffer, *The God Who Is There*, InterVarsity Press.)
Christianity is not relevant.	It is not relevant to *me* in *my* life. It is not practical; . . . it's "pie in the sky, by and by."	True Christianity is relevant and practical. The Bible is concerned with *all* of life, and not just with "*soul saving.*" This person has been exposed to defective forms of Christianity.
We are all a part of God. We are all children of God.	This person assumes that "ultimate reality," is of one being, and that man is part of this "world soul," or "cosmic force." It ends up in *pantheism* (all is God, God is all), or "paneverythingism" (all is Mind/Energy; Mind/Energy is all).	We are not a part of God. "God" is the personal, infinite Being who created this universe, not out of His own essence or being, but *out of nothing*. The Creator is qualitatively and quantitatively distinct from the creation. Pantheism and "Paneverythingism" lead to loss of identity and despair.
I try to keep the golden rule. I don't kick my neighbor when he is down. I do the best I can.	This statement is based on the assumption that God's acceptance of us depends on our person and performance. God will grade "on a curve" on the Judgment Day. If your good deeds outweigh your bad deeds, you will be all right!	God accepts sinners on the basis of the person and performance of Christ. Christianity is the only religion with a substitutionary atonement. We can never *work* our way to heaven. There is no "scale" to measure our good and bad deeds, for either salvation or condemnation. Salvation is by *grace alone*, through faith alone, in Christ alone! (Eph. 2:8, 9).

164

SURFACE OBJECTIONS	PRESUPPOSITIONS	CHRISTIAN ANSWERS
But, Christians are against sex. What's wrong with sex? It is natural, so it is right!	They assume: What is, is normal. What is normal, is right. THEREFORE, what is, is *right*. Also . . . "If it feels good, *do it*."	The fall of man into sin and guilt has made man subnormal and the world abnormal. What is, is *not* normal. We have desires which are *natural* to our fallen nature, but not *normal* to human nature as it was originally created. Sex is not wrong if it is "normal," i.e., if it is practiced where and when God originally planned.
I tried Christianity once, and it didn't work for me.	Christianity is an emotional "high" which does not last. There is no "real" conversion experience. Because their conversion was false, *all* are false. They judge everyone else by their own experience.	It is possible to have a false conversion experience. Whatever they tried, it was not real! However, one false conversion does not make *all* conversions false. This is not logically defensible, and does not correspond to reality.
Science has disproved the Bible. I believe in science.	Science and scientists are "neutral" and "objective," with no prejudices or presuppositions. Scientific *theories* are *always based on facts.*	Science continually changes its theories according to the presuppositions of the culture in which it exists. Science is not "neutral," or "objective." The scientist is controlled by his presuppositions, as well as his world and life view. Scientists make mistakes and produce false theories. As a matter of historical record, scientific *facts* have never disproved one word of Scripture. The theories of various scientists may contradict Scripture, but there is no evidence against Scripture.

SURFACE OBJECTIONS	PRESUPPOSITIONS	CHRISTIAN ANSWERS
Christianity is too narrow.	The best religion is one which makes everyone happy and secure. It assures all that everything is "going to be all right." *No religion should offend people by saying that it is the only true religion.*	Logically, since all religions contradict each other, there are only two options open to us. Either they are *all* false, or there is only *one* true religion. If there is only one God, there will be only *one* religion. The person who objects is "too narrow" to accept the truth.
I can't believe a loving God would send people to hell!	God is too good and man is too good for God to send man to hell. This person assumes that God thinks, feels and acts as *man* does. "If *I* would not send people to hell, neither would God!"	God is not a man. Neither does God think, feel, or act as a man would. His ways and thoughts are above ours. The real problem is that this person wants a "god" created in his own image— a "god" he can live with comfortably, while sinning. God loves justice, holiness, and righteousness *so much* that He created hell. The love of God for His own nature, His law, His universe, and His people makes hell a product of love as well as justice.
It doesn't matter what you believe as long as you are sincere.	Sincerity is more important than truth or morality.	This is not logically or morally defensible. No one can live according to this belief. Who would excuse sincere Satanists, who make human sacrifices? Was not Hitler sincere in his belief that all Jews should be exterminated? Sincerity cannot displace truth or morality; you can be sincerely *wrong* and also *sincerely immoral!*
Everything is relative. There are no absolutes.	Everything is relative *to the speaker's mind!* Man is the measure of all things. Might makes right. They assume that no moral judgments can be made on anyone for anything.	This statement is self-refuting. To say, "Everything is relative," or, "There are no absolutes," is to give an absolute statement which is not to be taken in a relative way! The statement is also unlivable. Hitler and child rapists would have to be approved. No moral judgments could be given. But, *all* people make moral judgments. No one can escape this aspect of life.

SURFACE OBJECTIONS	PRESUPPOSITIONS	CHRISTIAN ANSWERS
I can't believe in God. When I see what Hitler did to the Jews . . . and seeing all the pain and suffering in the world, I cannot believe there is a God.	We *can* make a moral condemnation of people, such as Hitler, without an absolute standard of morality and ethics. "God" is not necessary for making moral judgments.	The statement is not logically defensible. If there is no God, there is no absolute standard of morality and no basis for "justice." The problem of evil requires the existence of God. It does *not* negate God. The statement is also unlivable. The existence of God is essential to discern evil in order to condemn it. Without God, there is no "evil" *or* "good."
Evolution is true. We can't believe in the Bible anymore.	Evolution is "fact" and not *theory*. All evidence supports it. There is no evidence to prove creation. All scientists believe in evolution. No intelligent person can disagree with evolution. It is the best rational explanation of the universe. Creation is only a belief, a superstition.	Evolution is a mixed bag of many different, conflicting theories. Evolutionary theories are *theories* put forth by *some* scientists. None of these theories stand up to a rigorous scientific or philosophical examination. Creation has the evidence, while evolution has only a dogmatic faith. See Shute, *Flaws in the Theory of Evolution* (Presbyterian & Reformed Publishing Co.), for a rigorous scientific refutation of evolutionary theories.
The church is full of hypocrites.	Hypocrites receive God's blessings and will go to heaven when they die. All Christians must be perfect! One slip, and they are hypocrites. There are no hypocrites in the bars, discos, or business world. The person giving the objection assumes that he/she is *not* a hypocrite.	All hypocrites are condemned by God, according to Matthew 23:13, 33. Isn't it better to put up with them in the church for a few years instead of spending eternity in hell with them? Christianity is a "sinner's religion." It is wrong to think that Christians have to be perfect. Besides, there are hypocrites in every organization and group within society. Look to *Christ* to become a Christian! Christians may fail you, but Christ never fails.

167

SURFACE OBJECTIONS	PRESUPPOSITIONS	CHRISTIAN ANSWERS
All religions are the same. All roads lead to God. They all worship the same God. It is unkind to say that Christianity is *the* way to God!	They assume that if there is a God, He does not care what people think of Him, or how He should be worshiped. This "God" never revealed himself to man, or made His will known. Also, they assume that all religions teach the same doctrines about "God," "Sin," "World," "Man," and "Salvation." If they *do* all teach the same things, Christianity is then only *one* way among many ways.	God has revealed His own nature, and how He is to be worshiped. Christianity stands unique and apart from all other religions by its doctrines. Each religion has its own "God" or "god." The Christian Bible, and the religion which flows from it, is the only way to God that *God* has revealed! Jesus Christ is the only way to God (John 14:6). It is not unkind to tell people the truth lovingly.
Christianity is not rational or logical.	Most people actually mean their *own* "common sense" when they use the words "logic," or "reason." They are victims of thinking that reality must be whatever they *think* it to be. If something is not "logical" to *them*, they assume it cannot exist.	If you begin with your *reason* or *common sense* as the absolute authority, you end in skepticism. Usually the people who make this objection have faulty views of Christianity: i.e., a straw man of their own making. The Christian system is in accord with the Law of Contradiction. (See G. Clark, *Religion, Reason, and Revelation* (Presbyterian & Reformed Publishing Co.), for a logical demonstration of Christianity.)

168

SURFACE OBJECTIONS	PRESUPPOSITIONS	CHRISTIAN ANSWERS
What about the heathen?	The heathen have never received any revelation from God. The heathen are not to be viewed or treated as sinners, because they are ignorant. They are "noble savages." We are "lost" when we reject Christianity . . . but since they don't know anything about it, they can't be "lost" for rejecting it.	The heathen are lost because they are sinners, who have transgressed the general revelation found in the conscience and in the creation. They are "without excuse," according to Romans 1:20, and under condemnation (Rom. 2:12). We are lost because of what we *are*, not because of what we *know*.

Bibliography

A Modern Introduction to Philosophy. Eds. Paul Edwards and Arthur Pap. New York: Free Press,1965.

Aeschliman, Michael. *The Restitution of Man: C.S. Lewis and the Case Against Scientism.* Grand Rapids: Eerdmans, 1983.

Allis, Oswald. *The Five Books of Moses.* Phillipsburg, N.J.: Presbyterian and Reformed Pub. Co., 1964.

Altizer, Thomas J.J. *The Gospel of Christian Atheism.* Philadelphia: Westminster Press, 1966.

An Anthology of Atheism and Rationalism. Ed. Gordon Stein. Buffalo, N.Y.: Prometheus Books, 1984.

Anderson, Norman. *A Lawyer Among the Theologians.* Grand Rapids: Eerdmans, 1973.

————. *Jesus Christ: The Witness of History.* Downers Grove, Ill.: InterVarsity Press, 1985.

Angeles, Peter A. *Critiques of God.* Buffalo, N.Y.: Prometheus Books, 1976.

Bakunin, Michael. *God and the State.* New York: Freeport Press, n.d.

Balfour, Arthur James. *The Foundations of Belief.* New York: Longmans, Green, and Co., 1895.

Beckwith, B. *Religion, Philosophy, and Science.* New York: Philosophical Library, 1969.

Bentley, Richard. *Eight Boyle Lectures on Atheism.* New York: Garland Pub., 1976.

Beversluis, John. *C.S. Lewis and the Search for Rational Religion.* Grand Rapids: Eerdmans, 1984.

"Bible Errancy." Ed. Dennis McKinsey. Enon, Ohio.

Biblical Principles Concerning Issues of Importance to Godly Christians. Plymouth, Mass.: Plymouth Rock Foundation, 1984.

Blaiklock, E.M. *Jesus Christ: Man or Myth?* Nashville: Thomas Nelson, 1974.

Borne, Etienne. *Atheism*. New York: Hawthorn Books, 1961.

Brown, Colin. *Miracles and the Critical Mind*. Grand Rapids: Eerdmans, 1984.

Bruce, F.F. *Jesus and Christian Origins Outside the New Testament*. Grand Rapids: Eerdmans, 1974.

———. *The Defence of the Gospel in the New Testament*. Grand Rapids: Eerdmans, 1959.

Budd, Susan. *Varieties of Unbelief*. New York: Holmes and Meier Pubs., 1977.

Burkle, Howard R. *The Non-existence of God; Antitheism from Hegel to Dumery*. New York: Herder and Herder, 1969.

Capaldi, Nicholas. *The Art of Deception*. Buffalo, N.Y.: Prometheus Books, 1979.

Carnell, Edward J. *Christian Commitment: An Apologetic*. New York: Macmillan, 1957.

Carter, Lee. *Lucifer's Handbook*. Van Nuys: Academic Associates, 1977.

Cell, Edward. *Language, Existence and God*. Nashville: Abingdon Press, 1971.

Clark, Gordon. *Behaviorism and Christianity*. Jefferson, Md.: Trinity Foundation,1982.

———. *Dewey*. Phillipsburg, N.J.: Presbyterian and Reformed Pub. Co., 1960.

———. *Historiography: Secular and Religious*. New Jersey: Craig Press, 1971.

———. *Language and Theology*. Phillipsburg, N.J.: Presbyterian and Reformed Pub. Co., 1980.

———. *Religion, Reason and Revelation*. Phillipsburg, N.J.: Presbyterian and Reformed Pub. Co., 1961.

———. *Three Types of Religious Philosophy*. New Jersey: Craig Press, 1973.

———. *William James*. Phillipsburg, N.J.: Presbyterian and Reformed Pub. Co., 1963.

Classics of Free Thought. Ed. Paul Blanshard. Buffalo, N.Y.: Prometheus Books, n.d.

Collins, James D. *God in Modern Philosophy*. St. Louis University Press, 1959.

Copi, Irving. *Introduction to Logic*. N.Y.: MacMillan, 1981.

Copleston, Frederick. *Contemporary Philosophy*. Maryland: Newman Press, 1966.

Cosgrove, Michael. *The Essence of Man*. Grand Rapids: Zondervan, 1977.

"Creation/Evolution." Ed. Frederick Edwards. Buffalo, N.Y.

Cudworth, Ralph. *The True Intellectual System of the Universe*. Ed. Rene Wellek. New York: Garland Pub., 1978.

The Culture of Unbelief. Eds. Rocco Caporale and Antonio Grumelli.

Berkeley: University of California Press, 1971.

Davis, Stephen T. *Logic and the Nature of God*. Grand Rapids: Eerdmans, 1983.

De Bona, Maurice, Jr. *God Rejected*. Desserco Pub., 1976.

Dumery, Henry. *The Problem of God in Philosophy of Religion*. Northwestern Univ. Pr., 1964.

The Encyclopedia Americana.

The Encyclopedia of Philosophy. Ed. Paul Edwards. New York: Macmillan, 1977.

Encyclopedia of Unbelief. Buffalo, N.Y.: Prometheus Books, 1985.

Estrada, David and William White, Jr. *The First New Testament*. Nashville: Thomas Nelson, 1978.

Ewing, Alfred C. *A Short Commentary on Kant's Critique of Pure Reason*. University of Chicago Press, 1938.

Fabro, Cornelio. *God in Exile*. Maryland: Newman Press, 1968.

Fielding, William John. *The Shackles of the Supernatural*. New York: Vantage Press, 1969.

Flew, Antony. *God: A Critical Inquiry*. LaSalle, Ill.: Open Court, 1984.

————. *The Presumption of Atheism and Other Philosophical Essays on God, Freedom, and Immortality*. New York: Barnes and Noble, 1976.

————. *God, Freedom and Immortality*. Buffalo, N.Y.: Prometheus Books, 1984.

"Free Inquiry." Ed. Paul Kutz. Published by The Council for Democratic and Secular Humanism (CODESH, Inc.).

Gardavsky, Vitezslav. *God Is Not Yet Dead*. Harmondsworth: Peguin, 1973.

Gibson, Arthur. *The Faith of the Atheist*. New York: Harper and Row, 1968.

Gilbert, D. *Poison Peddlers*. Grand Rapids: Zondervan, n.d.

Graebner, Theodore Conrad. *God and the Cosmos*. Grand Rapids: Eerdmans, 1946.

Hagner, Donald A. *The Jewish Reclamation of Jesus*. Grand Rapids: Zondervan, 1984.

Hanna, Mark. *Crucial Questions in Apologetics*. Grand Rapids: Baker Book House, 1981.

Harrison, Roland Kenneth. *Archaeology of the New Testament*. New York: Association Press, 1964.

Harvey, Van A. *The Historian and the Believer*. New York: Macmillan, 1966.

Hastings, H. *Atheism and Arithmetic*. Hastings, 1885.

Hume, David. *Enquiry Concerning Human Understanding*. LaSalle, Ill.: Open Court, 1958.

Huxley, Julian S. *Religion Without Revelation*. New York: Harper, 1957.

Gorovitz, Samuel and Ron Williams. *Philosophical Analysis*. New York: Random House, 1966.

Griffin, Em. *The Mind Changers*. Wheaton, Ill.: Tyndale House, 1976.

Hick, John. *The Existence of God*. New York: Macmillan, 1964.

———. *Philosophy of Religion*. New York: Prentice-Hall, Inc., 1963.

Jastrow, Robert. *God and the Astronomers*. New York: W.W. Norton and Co., 1978.

Johnson, B.C. *The Atheist Debater's Handbook*. Buffalo, N.Y.: Prometheus Books, 1983.

Kim, Seyoon. *The Origin of Paul's Religion*. Grand Rapids: Eerdmans, 1981.

King's College Lectures on Immortality. London: University of London Press, 1920.

Kline, G. *Religious and Anti-religious Thought in Russia*. Chicago: University of Chicago, 1968.

Lacroix, Jean. *The Meaning of Modern Atheism*. New York: Macmillan, 1965.

Lepp, Ignace. *Atheism in Our Time*. New York: Macmillan, 1964.

Lewis, C.S. *Mere Christianity*. New York: Macmillan, 1960.

———. *Miracles*. New York: Macmillan, 1947.

———. *Surprised by Joy*. New York: Harcourt, Brace, Jovanovich, Inc., 1955.

———. *The Pilgrim's Regress*. London: Geoffery Bles, 1943.

Lewis, Gordon R. *Testing Christianity's Truth-Claims*. Chicago: Moody Press, 1976.

Lewis, Joseph. *The Bible Unmasked*. New York: Freethought Publishing Co., 1926.

Luypen, W. *Phenology and Atheism*. Duquesne University Press, 1964.

Machen, J. Gresham. *The Origin of Paul's Religion*. Grand Rapids: Eerdmans, 1925.

———. *The Virgin Birth of Christ*. New York: Harper and Brothers, 1930.

MacIntyre, Alasdair and Paul Ricceur. *The Religious Significance of Atheism*. New York: Columbia University Press, 1969.

Marshall, I. Howard. *I Believe in the Historical Jesus*. Grand Rapids: Eerdmans, 1977.

Masterson, Patrick. *Atheism and Alienation*. University of Notre Dame Press, 1971.

Marty, Martin. *The Infidel: Freethought and American Religion*. New York: Meridian Books, 1961.

———. *Varieties of Unbelief*. New York: Holt, Reinhart and Winston, 1969.

Matson, W. *The Existence of God*. Cornell University Press, 1965.

McDowell, Josh. *Evidence That Demands a Verdict*. San Bernardino, Cal.: Campus Crusade, 1972.

———. *More Than a Carpenter*. World Wide Pub., 1977.

———. *More Evidence That Demands a Verdict*. San Bernardino, Cal.: Campus Crusade, 1975.

McDowell, Josh and Don Stewart. *Answers to Tough Questions Skeptics Ask about the Christian Faith*. San Bernardino, Cal.: Campus Crusade, 1980.

———. *Understanding Secular Religions*. San Bernardino, Cal.: Here's Life Pub., 1982.

McGowan, Chris. *In the Beginning: A Scientist Shows Why the Creationists Are Wrong*. Buffalo, N.Y.: Prometheus Books, 1984.

Miceli, Vincent. *The Gods of Atheism*. Harrison, N.Y.: Roman Catholic Books Publishers, 1971.

Montgomery, John Warwick, *Christianity for the Tough Minded*. Minneapolis: Bethany House Publishers, 1973.

Morey, Robert. *Death and the Afterlife*. Minneapolis: Bethany House Publishers, 1984.

———. *A Christian Handbook for Defending the Faith*. Phillipsburg, N.J.: Presbyterian and Reformed Pub. Co., 1979.

Morris, Leon. *The Abolition of Religion*. Downers Grove, Ill.: InterVarsity, 1964.

Murray, William. *My Life Without God*. Nashville: Thomas Nelson, 1982.

Nash, Ronald. *Christianity and the Hellenistic World*. Grand Rapids: Zondervan, 1984.

———. *The Word of God and the Mind of Man*. Grand Rapids: Zondervan, 1982.

———. *The Concept of God*. Grand Rapids: Zondervan, 1983.

New Essays in Philosophical Theology. Eds. Anthony Flew and Alasdair MacIntyre. London: SCM Press, 1955.

Newman, Robert. *The Biblical Narratives of Easter Week: Are They Trustworthy?* Hatfield, Pa.: The Interdisciplinary Biblical Research Institute, 1979.

Nielsen, Kai. *Ethics Without God*. Buffalo, N.Y.: Prometheus Books, 1973.

O'Hair, Madalyn M. *What on Earth Is an Atheist?* New York: Arno Press, 1972.

Orr, James E. *Faith That Makes Sense*. Valley Forge, Pa.: Judson, 1960.

———. *100 Questions About God*. Glendale, Cal.: Regal Books, 1966.

Peace, Richard. *A Brief Bibliography for Young Atheists*. Downers Grove, Ill.: InterVarsity, 1969.

Penfield, Wilder. *The Mystery of the Mind*. Princeton: Princeton University Press, 1975.

Plantinga, Alvin. *God, Freedom, and Evil*. Grand Rapids: Eerdmans, 1974.

Popper, K.L. and J.C. Eccles. *Self and Its Brain*. New York: Springer-Verlag, 1977.

Purtill, Richard. *Reasons to Believe*. Grand Rapids: Eerdmans, 1974.

Ramm, Bernard. *Protestant Christian Evidences*. Chicago: Moody Press, 1953.

————. *The Christian View of Science and Scripture*. London: Patermaster Books, 1964.

————. *The God Who Makes a Difference*. Waco, Texas: Word, 1972.

Ramsey, Sir William Mitchell. *The Cities of St. Paul*. Grand Rapids: Baker Book House, 1960.

Recent Philosophy. Ed. Etienne Gilson. New York: Random House, 1962.

Reinach, Salomon. *Orpheus: A History of Religions*. New York: H. Liveright, Inc., 1932.

Reynolds, Vernon and Ralph E. Tanner. *The Biology of Religion*. White Plains: Longman, 1983.

Richards, W. *Reflections on French Atheism and English Christianity*. n.p., 1776.

Ridderbos, Herman. *Bultmann*. Phillipsburg, N.J.: Presbyterian and Reformed Pub. Co., 1960.

————. *Paul and Jesus*. Phillipsburg, N.J.: Presbyterian and Reformed Pub. Co., 1958.

Robinson, John A.T. *Redating the New Testament*. Philadelphia: Westminster Press, 1976.

Runes, Dagobert D. *Dictionary of Philosophy*. New Jersey: Littlefield, Adams and Co., 1967.

Rushdoony, Rousas. *Freud*. Phillipsburg, N.J.: Presbyterian and Reformed Pub. Co., 1965.

Russell, Bertrand. *Atheism: Collected Essays, 1943–1949*. New York: Arno Press, 1972.

————. *Why I Am Not a Christian*. New York: Arno Press, 1957.

Ryle, Gilbert. *The Concept of the Mind*. London: Oxford Press, 1949.

Samuel, Leith. *The Impossibility of Agnosticism*. Downers Grove, Ill.: InterVarsity, 1958.

Sanders, B. *Christianity After Freud*. Bles, 1949.

Schaeffer, Francis. *He Is There and He Is Not Silent*. Wheaton, Ill.: Tyndale, 1972.

————. *Genesis in Space and Time*. Downers Grove, Ill.: InterVarsity, 1972.

————. *The God Who Is There*. Downers Grove, Ill.: InterVarsity, 1968.

Schilling, Sylvester P. *God in an Age of Atheism*. Nashville: Abingdon Press, 1969.

Scientific Studies in Creation. Ed. William Edward Lammerts. Phillipsburg, N.J.: Presbyterian and Reformed Pub. Co., 1971.

Short, A. *Why Believe?* Downers Grove, Ill.: InterVarsity, 1962.

Smith, George H. *Atheism: The Case Against God*. Buffalo, N.Y.: Prometheus Books, 1979.

Sontag, Frederick. *The God of Evil*. New York: Harper and Row, 1970.

Sproul, Robert Charles. *Objections Answered*. Glendale, Cal.: Regal Books, 1978.

————. *The Pyschology of Atheism*. Minneapolis: Bethany House Publishers, 1974.

Sproul, Robert C., John Gestner, and Arthur Lindsley. *Classical Apologetics*. Grand Rapids: Zondervan, 1984.

Strunk, Orlo, Jr. *The Choice Called Atheism*. Nashville: Abingdon Press, 1969.

Sutherland, Stewart R. *Atheism and the Rejection of God*. Blackwell, 1977.

Swinburne, Richard. *The Coherence of Theism*. Clarendon Press, 1977.

Taylor, Kenneth. *Is Christianity Credible?* Downers Grove, Ill.: InterVarsity, 1970.

Taylor, Richard. *Metaphysics*. New York: Prentice-Hall, Inc., 1963.

Thrower, J. *A Short History of Western Atheism*. Buffalo, N.Y.: Prometheus Books, 1975.

Tourneur, Cyril. *The Atheist's Tragedy*. Harvard University Press, 1964.

Winchell, Paul. *God 2000: Religion Without the Bible*. Sylmar, Cal.: April Enterprizes, 1982.

Windelband, Wilhelm. *A History of Philosophy*. New York: Harper and Row, 1958.

Wurmbrand, Richard. *My Answer to the Moscow Atheists*. New Rochelle, N.Y.: Arlington House, 1975.

Yamauchi, Edwin M. *Pre-Christian Gnosticism: A Survey of the Proposed Evidences*. Grand Rapids: Baker Book House, 1983.

Zeller, Edward. *Outlines of the History of Greek Philosophy*. New York: Meridian Books, 1967.

Zukav, Gary. *Dancing Wu Li Masters: An Overview of the New Physics*. New York: Bantam Books, 1979.